Beyond Reality: The Rise of Digital Twins and Virtual Assets

SUMMARY

Chapter 1 - Introduction to Digital Twins.

Definition and Concepts	9
Historical Development	12
Benefits and Advantages	16
Current State of Technology	20

Chapter 2 - Applications in Manufacturing.

Process Optimization	27
Quality Control	31
Predictive Maintenance	35
Case Studies	39

Chapter 3 - Digital Twins in Construction.

Building Information Modeling (BIM)	45
Lifecycle Management	48
Safety Improvements	52

Future Possibilities   56

Chapter 4 - Supply Chain Management and Digital Twins.

Real-time Monitoring   61

Optimization Techniques   64

Risk Management   68

Integration with IoT   72

Chapter 5 - Advanced Analytics and Simulation.

Data Collection and Analysis   79

Simulation Models   82

Machine Learning Applications   86

Decision Support Systems   90

Chapter 6 - Technological Infrastructure.

Cloud Computing   97

Edge Computing   100

Networking Requirements — 104

Data Security — 108

Chapter 7 - Ethical and Privacy Considerations.

Data Ownership — 115

Privacy Concerns — 118

Ethical Frameworks — 122

Regulations and Compliance — 125

Chapter 8 - Future Trends and Opportunities.

Integration with AI — 131

Smart Cities — 134

Healthcare Innovations — 138

Sustainability Efforts — 142

Chapter 9 - Challenges and Limitations.

Technical Barriers — 149

Cost Considerations — 153

Adoption Hurdles   156

Interoperability Issues   160

Chapter 10 - Case Studies and Real-world Implementations.

Automotive Industry   167

Aerospace Applications   170

Energy Sector   174

Public Infrastructure   178

Chapter 1
Introduction to Digital Twins.

Definition and Concepts

In the rapidly evolving technological landscape, the concept of digital twins stands out as a fascinating and transformative innovation. Digital twins are virtual replicas of physical objects, systems, or processes, created to mirror the behaviors, characteristics, and dynamics of their real-world counterparts. These virtual models enable a comprehensive and detailed understanding of real-world objects and processes, facilitating monitoring, analysis, and optimization in ways that were previously unimaginable.

The genesis of digital twins can be traced back to the early 2000s, though the concept has gained significant traction in recent years due to advancements in computing power, data analytics, and the Internet of Things (IoT). At its core, a digital twin integrates real-time data from sensors, historical records, and domain knowledge to simulate the actual performance and behavior of physical entities. This integration provides an interactive bridge between the physical and digital realms, allowing for a level of insight and control that greatly enhances decision-making processes across various industries.

In manufacturing, digital twins have revolutionized how products are designed, tested, and maintained. Traditionally, developing a new product involved multiple iterations of physical prototypes, which were both time-consuming and costly. With digital twins, manufacturers can create virtual prototypes that undergo rigorous simulations and stress tests, identifying potential issues before any physical model is built. This approach not only accelerates the innovation process but also reduces costs and minimizes risks. Once a product is finalized and enters production, its digital twin continues to play a crucial role by monitoring real-time data from the factory floor, optimizing operations, and predicting maintenance needs.

Similarly, in the construction industry, digital twins are reshaping how buildings and infrastructure are designed and managed. Architects and engineers can create virtual models of structures, allowing them to evaluate various design scenarios, analyze energy efficiency, and optimize resource allocation. During the construction phase, digital twins enable real-time monitoring of progress, ensuring that projects stay on schedule and within budget. Once the project is completed, the digital twin serves as a dynamic, living model of the structure, providing valuable insights for facility management, maintenance, and future renovations.

The global supply chain is another area where digital twins are making a profound impact. Supply chain management involves coordinating a complex network of suppliers, manufacturers, logistics providers, and retailers. By deploying digital twins, companies can achieve a level of visibility and agility that was once unattainable. Real-time data from various points in the supply chain can be fed into digital twins to simulate different scenarios, forecast demand, and optimize inventory levels. This not only enhances efficiency but also improves the ability to respond to disruptions such as natural disasters, political instability, or sudden changes in market conditions.

As we look to the future, the potential applications of digital twins appear boundless. From healthcare, where digital twins of patients could revolutionize personalized medicine, to smart cities, where urban planning and infrastructure management could be optimized through virtual models, the scope for innovation is immense. However, as with any transformative technology, the rise of digital twins also brings forth ethical considerations that must be carefully navigated. Issues such as data privacy, security, and the potential displacement of jobs due to automation are crucial aspects that society must address to ensure that digital twin technology is deployed responsibly and equitably.

In summarizing the essence of digital twins, it becomes evident that these virtual counterparts are not merely futuristic fantasies but practical tools that are reshaping industries and redefining possibilities. By harnessing the power of data and simulation, digital twins provide a profound understanding of the physical world, ushering in an era of unprecedented efficiency, innovation, and transformative potential. As we continue to explore and refine this technology, it is imperative that we remain mindful of both its capabilities and its consequences, striving to leverage its benefits while safeguarding against its risks.

Historical Development

The historical development of digital twins is a

fascinating journey that stretches back several decades, tracing a path through the evolution of computer modeling and simulation technologies. The concept of creating virtual replicas of physical objects may seem like a product of the 21st century, but its roots reach much deeper into the history of technological innovation. Understanding this development helps to appreciate how digital twins have grown from theoretical ideas into practical, transformative tools in various industries.

In the mid-20th century, the rapid advancement of computing technology laid the groundwork for the digital twin concept. The emergence of powerful computers enabled engineers and scientists to simulate physical processes and create mathematical models of real-world systems. This period saw the birth of early computer-aided design (CAD) programs, which allowed for the creation of digital models used primarily in engineering and architectural design. These developments were revolutionary, significantly enhancing precision, reducing errors, and lowering costs in construction and manufacturing.

Moving into the 1980s and 1990s, the concept of

simulation took on a new dimension with the advent of more sophisticated software and better processing power. Researchers began to explore the idea of creating dynamic models that were not static representations but could simulate real-time behaviors and responses of physical systems. This era marked the beginning of more intensive explorations into what would eventually lead to the digital twin paradigm. For instance, NASA's use of mirror systems during the Apollo missions can be considered an early form of digital twinning. Engineers created exact replicas of spacecraft on Earth to diagnose problems and devise solutions simultaneously with real-time issues encountered in space.

The 2000s brought about significant conceptual advancements. The term "digital twin" itself was coined by Dr. Michael Grieves in 2002 during his presentation at a Society of Manufacturing Engineers conference. He envisioned a twin born from the synergy of the physical and virtual world, describing a model that could help in manufacturing and product lifecycle management by providing a continuous loop of real-time data updates and simulations. Grieves' work laid the intellectual foundation for the formal adoption and extensive exploration of digital twins.

During the late 2000s and early 2010s, digital twins began to gain traction in various industries beyond manufacturing. The development of the Internet of Things (IoT) played a crucial role in this expansion. The IoT enabled the connection of physical objects to the internet, allowing for real-time data collection and communication. This capability allowed digital twins to be more accurate and reflective of current states of their physical counterparts. Industries such as healthcare, urban planning, and asset management started to experiment with and implement digital twins, leveraging these advancements to optimize operations, reduce downtimes, and create predictive maintenance schedules.

In recent years, the convergence of technologies such as artificial intelligence, machine learning, and advanced analytics has dramatically enhanced the capabilities of digital twins. These technologies enable more sophisticated simulations, predictive analytics, and near-autonomous management of complex systems. Today, digital twins are not only capable of representing and simulating physical entities but can also integrate their contexts and environments, thereby offering a holistic view of entire ecosystems. This evolution has been especially transformative in industries like aerospace, where digital twins are used to manage the lifecycle of aircraft, and in smart cities, where they help to optimize traffic flows, energy use, and urban planning.

Thus, the journey of digital twins over the decades showcases a remarkable story of technological progression. From rudimentary simulations and static models to the dynamic, interconnected virtual replicas of today, digital twins have become indispensable elements of modern industry. As we continue to innovate and integrate new technologies, the potential for digital twins will only grow, promising to bring even greater efficiencies and advancements across various sectors.

Benefits and Advantages

The concept of digital twins has rapidly gained traction across various industries, revolutionizing traditional methods and unlocking new levels of efficiency, innovation, and precision. At its core, a digital twin is a virtual replica of a physical asset, object, or system that offers unprecedented insights and control over its real-world counterpart. The benefits and advantages of implementing digital twins are manifold, spanning from enhanced operational efficiencies to groundbreaking advancements in sustainability and resilience.

One of the foremost benefits of digital twins lies in their ability to optimize operations through real-time monitoring and predictive analytics. By continuously mirroring the state of the physical asset, digital twins allow for constant surveillance and adjustments. This real-time data collection and analysis enable operators to identify performance bottlenecks, foresee potential failures, and implement corrective measures before they escalate into costly downtimes or malfunctions. The predictive maintenance facilitated by digital twins not only extends the lifespan of machinery and equipment but also translates into significant cost savings and enhanced productivity.

Furthermore, digital twins play a pivotal role in fostering innovation and improving the design and development process of products. Engineers and designers can simulate various scenarios and conditions using the digital twin, experimenting with different design parameters and operational conditions without incurring the costs or risks associated with physical prototypes. This ability to virtually test and optimize designs accelerates the innovation cycle, leading to faster time-to-market and higher-quality products. The iterative feedback loop created by digital twins ensures continual refinement and enhancement, driving both efficiency and creativity in product development.

In the realm of supply chain management, digital twins contribute to increased transparency and agility. By providing a holistic view of the entire supply chain, from raw material sourcing to end-user delivery, digital twins enable stakeholders to monitor and manage each link in the chain with unparalleled precision. This visibility allows for the identification and mitigation of disruptions, better inventory management, and more accurate demand forecasting. The enhanced coordination and responsiveness afforded by digital twins lead to a more resilient and adaptable supply chain, capable of swiftly responding to market fluctuations and unforeseen challenges.

Sustainability is another critical area where digital twins have significant implications. By optimizing resource utilization and reducing waste, digital twins support environmentally friendly practices. For instance, in manufacturing, digital twins can streamline production processes to minimize energy consumption and material waste. In construction, they can assist in designing more energy-efficient buildings by simulating various environmental conditions and evaluating the performance of different materials and designs. The data-driven insights provided by digital twins promote sustainable practices, contributing to broader efforts to reduce the environmental impact of industrial activities.

Moreover, digital twins enhance decision-making at all levels of an organization by providing a comprehensive and accurate representation of physical assets and processes. The integration of artificial intelligence and machine learning algorithms with digital twin models further amplifies their analytical capabilities, offering predictive and prescriptive insights that inform strategic and operational decisions. Decision-makers are equipped with a robust tool that supports evidence-based planning and execution, driving better outcomes and more informed strategies in an increasingly complex and competitive landscape.

In conclusion, the advantages of digital twins extend far beyond mere digital replicas; they are transformative tools that enhance operational efficiency, foster innovation, strengthen supply chain resilience, and promote sustainability. The integration of digital twins into various sectors is not just a technological upgrade but a paradigm shift, enabling a more connected, efficient, and intelligent approach to managing and optimizing physical assets and processes. As industries continue to embrace and expand the applications of digital twins, the potential for further advancements and benefits is boundless, heralding a new era of digital transformation and progress.

Current State of Technology

In the current state of technology, digital twins have emerged as a groundbreaking innovation with immense potential across various industries. At its core, a digital twin is a virtual replica of a physical object, system, or process. This concept, which once seemed like a notion from science fiction, has now become a tangible reality thanks to the advancements in data analytics, the Internet of Things (IoT), artificial intelligence (AI), and machine learning (ML).

The integration of IoT devices is a critical enabler for the development and deployment of digital twins. Sensors embedded within physical objects continuously gather data, providing real-time information about their status, performance, and environment. This data is then transmitted to a digital platform where the digital twin resides. By leveraging AI and ML algorithms, the digital twin can process this influx of data, offering insights that are not only precise but also predictive. These technologies enable the digital twin to simulate the physical counterpart's behavior under various conditions, predict potential failures, and optimize performance with incredible accuracy.

Manufacturing is one of the leading industries benefiting from digital twin technology. Factories equipped with digital twins can visualize and simulate entire production processes, from the intricate functioning of machinery to the flow of materials. This not only improves operational efficiency but also allows manufacturers to identify bottlenecks, predict equipment failures before they occur, and streamline maintenance schedules. Consequently, production downtime is minimized, and overall productivity is significantly enhanced. Moreover, the digital twin of a product can be used to monitor its performance throughout its lifecycle, from the factory floor to the end-user, providing valuable feedback for future product improvements.

In the construction and infrastructure sectors, digital twins are revolutionizing how projects are designed, built, and maintained. Building Information Modeling (BIM) systems serve as the foundation for creating digital twins of buildings and infrastructure. These twins provide an interactive, 3D representation of physical structures, allowing for real-time monitoring and management. Engineers and architects can simulate various scenarios, such as structural stress or environmental impact, to identify potential issues before they manifest in the real world. This predictive capability leads to safer, more efficient construction practices and ensures longevity and durability of the infrastructure.

Supply chain management is another area where digital twins are making significant strides. By creating digital replicas of the entire supply chain, from raw materials to customer delivery, companies gain unprecedented visibility and control. These digital twins enable the monitoring of inventory levels, tracking of shipments, and prediction of potential disruptions due to unforeseen events like natural disasters or geopolitical tensions. The result is a more resilient, responsive, and efficient supply chain capable of adapting to dynamic market conditions.

The healthcare industry also stands to gain from the implementation of digital twin technology. Patient-specific digital twins are being developed, which can model the unique biological systems of individuals. These twins can simulate disease progression, predict responses to various treatments, and assist in personalized medicine. By providing doctors and researchers with a comprehensive understanding of an individual's health, digital twins open new avenues for preventive care and tailored medical interventions.

Despite the promising advancements, the adoption

of digital twins is not without challenges. Issues related to data privacy, cybersecurity, and the ethical considerations of digital replicas must be meticulously addressed. Ensuring the integrity and security of the data feeding digital twins is paramount, as is handling the implications of such detailed simulations.

The current state of digital twin technology is both exciting and evolving. As these virtual replicas continue to integrate into various sectors, they foster a new era of innovation and efficiency, paving the way for a future where the physical and digital realms are seamlessly interconnected.

Chapter 2
Applications in Manufacturing.

Process Optimization

Process optimization in manufacturing is one of the most compelling applications of digital twins. This technology holds the promise of transforming how factories operate, offering unprecedented insights and control over each step of production. Through the creation of virtual replicas of physical assets—be it machines, production lines, or entire facilities—manufacturers can monitor performance in real-time, diagnose problems faster, and enhance overall efficiency in ways previously unimaginable.

The integration of digital twins into manufacturing processes allows for a more nuanced and comprehensive understanding of operations. By mirroring the physical production environment in a digital space, companies can simulate different scenarios without disrupting actual workflows. This capability is particularly beneficial for identifying bottlenecks, optimizing resource allocation, and predicting maintenance needs. For instance, a digital twin of a production line can replicate the behavior of every machine and sensor involved, enabling predictive maintenance by identifying potential points of failure before they become critical issues. This preemptive approach reduces downtime and extends the lifespan of machinery, ultimately saving costs and boosting productivity.

Moreover, digital twins facilitate continuous improvement in manufacturing processes. Through constant data collection and analysis, these virtual models offer a feedback loop that informs adjustments and improvements in real-time. Any deviation from expected performance metrics can be swiftly addressed, whether it involves fine-tuning the operation of a single machine or reconfiguring an entire workflow. In essence, digital twins serve as a dynamic blueprint of the factory floor, continuously updating to reflect the most efficient methods of production. This adaptability ensures that processes remain as streamlined and cost-effective as possible.

The ability to simulate and analyze various operational strategies also supports innovation in product development. Digital twins enable manufacturers to prototype and test new products in a virtual environment before committing resources to physical production. This not only accelerates the development cycle but also minimizes the risks associated with introducing new products to the market. By foreseeing potential issues and optimizing designs digitally, companies can ensure higher quality and reliability in their final products.

Additionally, digital twins enhance collaboration across different departments within a manufacturing organization. Engineers, operators, and managers can all access the same up-to-date virtual representation of the factory floor, facilitating better communication and decision-making. This shared understanding helps in coordinating efforts, whether it's troubleshooting a malfunctioning piece of equipment or implementing new production strategies. The result is a more cohesive and responsive manufacturing operation.

The environmental impact of manufacturing can also be mitigated through the use of digital twins. By optimizing processes and reducing waste, manufacturers can lower their carbon footprint and operate more sustainably. Virtual simulations help identify the most energy-efficient production methods, and predictive maintenance reduces the need for frequent replacements of machinery, thereby decreasing material consumption. In this way, digital twins contribute to more eco-friendly manufacturing practices.

Ethically, the deployment of digital twins must be done with consideration for workers' roles and data privacy. While automation and optimization can enhance efficiency, they should not come at the expense of job security or personal privacy. Transparent policies and inclusive training programs can ensure that employees understand and benefit from new technologies rather than being displaced by them.

In conclusion, digital twins represent a paradigm shift in manufacturing, offering tools to optimize processes, reduce costs, and innovate effectively. By leveraging real-time data and sophisticated simulations, manufacturers can achieve higher efficiency and sustainability while maintaining competitive advantage. As this technology continues to evolve, it promises to further revolutionize how we understand and execute manufacturing operations, leading to smarter, more adaptable industrial practices.

Quality Control

In the realm of manufacturing, digital twins have revolutionized quality control processes, ushering in an era where defects and inefficiencies can be identified and rectified with unprecedented precision. The concept of digital twins in quality control pivots on creating a virtual model of a physical asset, enabling real-time monitoring and analysis. This synergy between the physical and digital worlds allows for a proactive approach to quality assurance, significantly reducing the margin for error and enhancing overall product quality.

At the heart of this transformation lies the ability of digital twins to simulate and predict performance. By continuously gathering data from sensors embedded in physical assets, digital twins generate a real-time virtual representation of these assets. This dynamic model enables manufacturers to conduct in-depth analyses without interrupting the production process. Any deviation from the predefined parameters can be detected instantly, allowing for immediate corrective actions. For instance, in the automotive industry, digital twins of engine components can monitor temperature, pressure, and other critical factors to ensure they remain within optimal ranges, thereby preventing potential failures.

One of the paramount advantages of utilizing digital twins in quality control is the capacity for predictive maintenance. Traditional maintenance schedules often operate on a fixed timeline, which can result in either premature maintenance, wasting resources, or delayed interventions, leading to equipment failure. Digital twins obviate this issue by predicting when and where maintenance is needed, based on real-time data. This predictive capability minimizes downtime and extends the lifespan of machinery, ensuring that the production line runs smoothly and efficiently.

Furthermore, digital twins facilitate a deeper understanding of the manufacturing process, unveiling areas where improvements can be implemented. By simulating different scenarios and stress-testing the virtual model, manufacturers can foresee how changes in the production process might impact product quality. This ability to test and refine processes in a virtual environment not only reduces the risk associated with implementing changes in the physical world but also expedites the innovation cycle. For example, a pharmaceutical company can utilize digital twins to simulate the effects of varying temperatures and humidity levels during drug manufacturing, ensuring consistent product quality and compliance with regulatory standards.

The integration of artificial intelligence and machine learning with digital twins further amplifies their efficacy in quality control. These technologies enable digital twins to learn from historical data and improve their predictive accuracy over time. By recognizing patterns and anomalies, AI-driven digital twins can offer insights that were previously unattainable. This intelligent analysis accelerates decision-making processes and empowers manufacturers to implement data-driven quality control measures swiftly and effectively.

Moreover, digital twins foster a collaborative environment by providing a unified platform where stakeholders can access and analyze data in real-time. This transparency ensures that everyone, from engineers to quality control inspectors, operates with the same information, fostering cohesive decision-making. Through cloud-based access, teams can monitor the production process remotely, facilitating timely interventions and maintaining continuity in operations, especially in a globalized supply chain.

Ethical considerations accompany the deployment of digital twins in quality control. Ensuring data privacy and security is paramount, as the vast amounts of data generated must be protected from cyber threats. Moreover, there is a need to address the potential displacement of workers due to increased automation. Upskilling and reskilling initiatives are essential to prepare the current workforce for the evolving digital landscape, ensuring that human expertise complements technological advancements.

In conclusion, digital twins are transforming quality control in manufacturing by providing an intricate, real-time virtual representation of physical assets. Through predictive maintenance, process optimization, AI integration, and enhanced collaboration, these technologies are setting new benchmarks for product quality and operational efficiency. As the manufacturing landscape continues to evolve, the adoption and ethical deployment of digital twins will be crucial in shaping a future where quality and innovation go hand in hand.

Predictive Maintenance

Predictive maintenance is one of the most revolutionary applications of digital twins in the manufacturing industry. By creating a virtual replica of physical machinery, manufacturers can monitor and analyze equipment in real-time, ensuring that any potential issues are identified and addressed before they result in costly downtime or catastrophic failures. The efficiency and predictive power of digital twins transform the static nature of traditional maintenance schedules into a dynamic and responsive system.

The process begins with data collection through various sensors embedded in the physical assets. These sensors gather continuous streams of information on parameters such as temperature, vibration, and pressure. This data is then fed into the digital twin, a virtual model that mirrors the operational and physical attributes of the machinery. Through sophisticated algorithms and machine learning, the digital twin can simulate various scenarios and predict future behavior based on current and historical data.

One of the primary benefits of predictive maintenance powered by digital twins is the ability to anticipate failures before they occur. For instance, a rise in vibration levels might not be immediately noticeable but could signify impending bearing failure. The digital twin, designed to recognize such patterns, can alert maintenance teams to anomalies, prompting timely inspections and interventions. This proactive approach allows for repairs or part replacements to occur during scheduled downtimes, significantly reducing the risk of unexpected breakdowns and prolonging the machinery's lifespan.

Moreover, digital twins facilitate a more nuanced understanding of an asset's performance. Traditionally, maintenance schedules are based on estimations and manufacturer guidelines, often resulting in parts being replaced either too early or too late. With a digital twin, maintenance can be conducted precisely when necessary, optimizing the operational lifecycle of each component. This predictive accuracy leads to considerable cost savings, as resources are allocated efficiently and unnecessary replacements are avoided.

Another advantage lies in the improvement of safety standards. Malfunctioning equipment can pose significant risks not only to production lines but also to the safety of factory personnel. By identifying potential issues in advance, digital twins create a safer working environment. Ensuring machinery operates within optimal parameters reduces the likelihood of accidents and contributes to a culture of safety within the organization.

Furthermore, the data generated and analyzed by digital twins provides valuable insights for future designs and operational strategies. Manufacturers can discern patterns and correlations that may not have been evident otherwise. For instance, certain operational conditions might consistently lead to quicker wear and tear of machine parts. These findings can inform design improvements, preventive measures, and operating procedures that enhance overall efficiency and durability.

The integration of the Internet of Things (IoT) with

digital twins adds another layer of depth to predictive maintenance. IoT devices communicate with the digital twin in real-time, creating a continuous feedback loop that fine-tunes predictive models and ensures the most up-to-date information is being considered. This synergy accelerates the learning process for predictive algorithms, making predictions more accurate over time.

Despite these tremendous benefits, the implementation of digital twins for predictive maintenance is not without challenges. Ensuring data accuracy, maintaining cybersecurity, and integrating digital twin systems with existing infrastructure require substantial investment and expertise. However, the long-term gains in operational efficiency, cost savings, and safety far outweigh the initial hurdles, making digital twins an invaluable asset in modern manufacturing.

In summary, predictive maintenance through digital twins represents a significant leap forward for the manufacturing industry, transitioning from reactive to proactive management of machinery. By harnessing real-time data, advanced simulations, and machine learning, manufacturers can anticipate and address issues before they escalate, optimizing performance, reducing costs, and ensuring a safer working environment. As this technology continues to evolve, it promises to redefine the standards of efficiency and reliability in manufacturing operations globally.

Case Studies

One compelling case study in the realm of manufacturing involves General Electric (GE), a company that has been at the forefront of integrating digital twin technology into its industrial processes. GE started to develop detailed digital replicas of their jet engines and gas turbines. These digital twins are more than just static models; they are living representations updated in real-time with data from sensors on the actual machines. This transformation has revolutionized how GE approaches maintenance and operational efficiency. For instance, predictive maintenance is a game-changer, allowing engineers to foresee potential issues before they become critical problems. By analyzing the data from the digital twin, GE can predict when a component is likely to fail and preemptively replace it, thus avoiding costly downtime.

In another example, Siemens, a global powerhouse in industrial manufacturing, has utilized digital twins to enhance its product design and engineering processes. In their Amberg Electronics Plant, Siemens creates a digital twin of each product as well as the entire production process. By analyzing these digital replicas, Siemens can simulate different scenarios and optimize the manufacturing line. This not only accelerates the engineering cycle but also ensures higher quality and consistency in the final products. The digital twin allows engineers to tweak designs and production parameters in a virtual environment, mitigating risks and improving efficiency without the need for physical prototypes.

Similarly, in the automotive industry, Tesla has embraced digital twin technology to streamline its manufacturing and enhance vehicle performance. Each Tesla car has its digital twin that collects data in real-time from the physical vehicle. This data is diligently analyzed to monitor performance, detect anomalies, and provide insights into potential improvements. As a result, Tesla can continuously update its vehicle software, ensuring better functionality and driving experience for its customers. This iterative process of data collection and analysis facilitated by digital twins significantly reduces the time from conception to production, giving Tesla a competitive edge in innovation and market agility.

Another notable example is the Boeing Company, leveraging digital twins to optimize the production of its aerospace systems. Boeing employs digital twins to represent individual airplane parts and the entire assembly process. By simulating the manufacturing process, Boeing can identify potential bottlenecks, streamline assembly lines, and enhance productivity. These virtual models are also critical in testing new designs and materials under various simulated conditions, reducing the time and cost associated with physical testing.

Moreover, in the pharmaceutical manufacturing sector, GlaxoSmithKline (GSK) has pioneered the use of digital twins to optimize their production processes. GSK has created digital twins for some of their production lines, enabling them to simulate and optimize the manufacturing of complex biological drugs. These simulations help in identifying the optimal conditions for production, reducing waste, and ensuring consistency in drug quality. By providing a detailed understanding of the manufacturing process through virtual replicas, GSK can achieve higher levels of efficiency and reliability in their production pipelines.

The integration of digital twins in manufacturing is not just a technological advancement; it represents a paradigm shift in how products are designed, produced, and maintained. These case studies illustrate the transformative potential of digital twins, not only in improving operational efficiencies but also in fostering innovation and sustainability. The ability to create virtual models that evolve with their physical counterparts paves the way for a more agile, responsive, and intelligent manufacturing landscape. As these technologies continue to advance, the boundaries between the digital and physical worlds will further blur, heralding a new era of industrial excellence.

Chapter 3
Digital Twins in Construction.

Building Information Modeling (BIM)

Building Information Modeling (BIM) has become a cornerstone in the construction industry, revolutionizing the way projects are designed, constructed, and managed. This advanced digital representation integrates multi-dimensional data about a building project into a cohesive, interactive model that can be used throughout the lifecycle of a construction project, from the initial design phase to operation and maintenance.

At its core, BIM is not just about creating a 3D model; it's about fostering a collaborative environment where architects, engineers, and construction professionals can access, share, and update information in real-time. This collaboration is crucial for identifying potential issues before they arise, streamlining workflows, and ultimately reducing costs. By simulating the physical and functional characteristics of a construction project, BIM software enables stakeholders to visualize the project in a virtual space, allowing for a more comprehensive understanding of the building's structure and components. This enhances decision-making processes and ensures everyone works from the same updated plans, minimizing the risk of costly errors and rework.

Incorporating the notion of digital twins into BIM takes this approach to an entirely new level. Digital twins are not static representations; they are dynamic, living models that evolve as changes occur in the actual physical world. In construction, this means that a digital twin can be continuously updated with real-time data from sensors embedded in the physical building, providing an accurate and up-to-date representation of the infrastructure. This affords an unparalleled level of insight and foresight, enabling predictive maintenance and more efficient facility management.

One of the most profound benefits of using BIM with digital twins in construction is the ability to enhance sustainability and energy efficiency. By simulating energy usage, lighting, and HVAC systems within the BIM environment, it becomes possible to test and optimize different scenarios before they are implemented in the real world. This can significantly reduce the environmental impact of buildings and contribute to the creation of smarter, greener cities. Furthermore, the integrated data within a BIM model can be used to track and improve the sustainability of materials and construction practices, aligning with global efforts to reduce carbon footprints.

Another compelling advantage of BIM in the context of digital twins is its impact on construction safety. By simulating construction tasks in a virtual environment, potential hazards can be identified and mitigated before they become real-world issues. This proactive approach to safety can substantially reduce the occurrence of accidents on construction sites, safeguarding workers and ensuring compliance with safety regulations. Additionally, real-time data from construction sites can be fed back into the BIM system to continually update the digital twin with the latest safety insights and incident reports.

While the potential of BIM combined with digital twins is immense, there are significant challenges to consider, particularly around data interoperability and standardization. Ensuring that all stakeholders can seamlessly exchange information without losing detail or accuracy requires robust frameworks and protocols. This necessitates ongoing collaboration between software developers, industry professionals, and regulatory bodies to create and maintain these standards.

In conclusion, Building Information Modeling is a transformative technology in the construction industry that provides a foundation for the integration of digital twins. This combination enhances collaborative efforts, boosts efficiency, improves sustainability, and ensures safer working environments. As these technologies continue to evolve, they hold the promise of making the construction industry not only more innovative but also more responsive to the needs of the future.

Lifecycle Management

Lifecycle management in the construction sector is a multifaceted domain that is significantly enhanced by the integration of digital twins. These virtual replicas serve as comprehensive models of their physical counterparts, capturing the minutiae from design inception through construction completion and beyond to facilities management. By enabling a continuous flow of real-time data, digital twins have redefined the traditional lifecycle management processes, bringing a spectrum of benefits that elevate efficiency, accuracy, and sustainability.

At the inception stage of a construction project, digital twins assist in refining design specifications by providing a dynamic and interactive representation of the future structure. Architects and engineers can input various parameters and instantly observe the impact of design choices on structural integrity, material use, and cost. This real-time feedback loop reduces the frequency of revisions, streamlining the planning phase and ensuring a higher degree of precision. The ability to simulate different design scenarios enables stakeholders to make informed decisions, fostering a more collaborative environment where designers, builders, and clients can converge on the optimal solution.

As the project transitions from design to construction, digital twins come to the forefront in orchestrating the complex choreography of activities on-site. These virtual models enable project managers to monitor construction progress in real time, comparing the evolving site conditions against the planned schedule. Any discrepancies can be quickly identified and addressed, mitigating the risks associated with delays and cost overruns. Moreover, the predictive capabilities of digital twins offer forewarnings about potential issues such as structural weaknesses or resource shortages, allowing proactive measures to be taken.

Furthermore, digital twins enhance quality assurance practices within construction. The virtual models serve as benchmarks for validating the conformity of the constructed elements to the original specifications. Quality control teams can conduct virtual inspections, employing augmented reality (AR) to visualize the digital twin overlaid on the physical structure. This ensures meticulous adherence to design and standards, significantly reducing the likelihood of defective workmanship and ensuring that safety protocols are uncompromised. As a result, the deployment of digital twins supports the delivery of projects on time and within budget, while also upholding the highest quality standards.

Upon completion of the construction phase, the functional utility of digital twins transcends into the realm of facilities management and operational maintenance. The same digital model that guided the construction process now serves as a living document of the built environment, chronicling every component and system within the structure. Facility managers can leverage this granular data to optimize maintenance schedules, track the performance of critical assets, and predict failures before they occur. By utilizing predictive maintenance techniques facilitated by the continuous data stream from the digital twin, facility managers can extend the lifespan of building systems and reduce the total cost of ownership.

Moreover, digital twins play a pivotal role in post-construction modifications and renovations. The comprehensive digital archives allow planners to simulate various renovation scenarios to assess feasibility and impact, facilitating efficient retrofitting processes. As buildings evolve to incorporate new technologies or adjust to changing needs, the digital twin remains an indispensable tool for managing these transitions seamlessly.

In conclusion, the implementation of digital twins in the construction sector revolutionizes traditional lifecycle management by providing an integrated, real-time, and data-rich perspective of the entire project journey. From design clarity and construction efficiency to superior quality control and proactive maintenance, digital twins ensure that every phase of the construction lifecycle is handled with unprecedented accuracy and insight. These benefits collectively represent a transformative leap towards a more intelligent, cohesive, and sustainable approach to building the world of tomorrow.

Safety Improvements

The advent of digital twins in the construction industry has ushered in a new era of safety improvements, transforming how projects are managed and ensuring that risks are minimized. By creating virtual replicas of physical structures, digital twins offer a multitude of opportunities for enhancing safety protocols and practices throughout the construction process.

At the heart of these improvements is the ability to simulate and analyze potential hazards before they become real-world problems. With a digital twin, construction managers can perform detailed risk assessments by virtually testing different scenarios.

This enables them to pinpoint weak spots in design and construction plans, allowing for modifications that enhance structural integrity and worker safety. For instance, a digital twin can help identify areas where workers might be at risk from falling debris or where structural weaknesses could lead to collapses. By addressing these issues in the virtual model, safety measures can be implemented in the physical project, reducing the likelihood of accidents.

Moreover, digital twins enable real-time monitoring of construction sites, providing a continuous stream of data that can be analyzed to preemptively address safety concerns. Sensors embedded in the physical structure feed data back to the digital twin, allowing for constant surveillance of the site's conditions. This data can reveal critical information, such as shifts in structural elements or changes in environmental conditions that could pose danger. For example, if a sensor detects abnormal vibrations in a crane, the digital twin can signal an alert, prompting immediate inspection and maintenance to prevent potentially catastrophic incidents.

Training and preparedness are also significantly enhanced through the use of digital twins. Safety training programs can leverage these virtual models to create immersive simulations that replicate real-world conditions and challenges. Workers can engage in lifelike scenarios where they practice responding to emergencies, navigating complex construction environments, and adhering to safety protocols. This hands-on experience, gained in a risk-free digital environment, prepares workers to handle actual on-site situations more effectively and safely. It also instills a deeper understanding and respect for safety measures, contributing to a culture of safety throughout the workforce.

Additionally, digital twins facilitate better communication and coordination among different teams and stakeholders involved in the construction project. When all parties have access to a shared, up-to-date digital twin, it ensures that everyone is on the same page regarding safety protocols and project status. This transparency reduces misunderstandings and errors that could lead to unsafe conditions. Collaboration tools integrated with digital twins enable quick dissemination of critical safety updates and instructions, ensuring rapid response to any emerging issues.

The predictive analytics capabilities of digital twins also play a pivotal role in enhancing safety. By harnessing the power of machine learning and AI, digital twins can forecast potential safety hazards based on past data and current trends. These predictions help construction managers make informed decisions about safety measures, resource allocation, and scheduling to mitigate risks. For instance, if predictive models indicate an increased likelihood of accidents due to projected weather conditions, proactive steps can be taken to protect workers and equipment, such as rescheduling tasks or reinforcing protective measures.

In conclusion, the integration of digital twins in the construction industry marks a significant leap forward in safety improvements. Through advanced simulations, real-time monitoring, immersive training, enhanced communication, and predictive analytics, digital twins provide a comprehensive framework for identifying, addressing, and preventing safety issues. As these technologies continue to evolve, they hold the promise of creating safer construction environments, protecting both workers and assets, and ultimately ensuring the successful and secure completion of construction projects.

Future Possibilities

As advancements in technology continue to shape the landscape of various industries, digital twins in construction hold immense potential for the future. With their ability to create precise virtual representations of physical structures, digital twins are set to revolutionize how we design, build, and manage construction projects. One of the most promising aspects lies in their capacity to enhance collaboration and streamline the decision-making process. By providing a single, centralized source of truth, digital twins allow all stakeholders to access up-to-date information in real time, fostering a more cohesive and informed project environment. This not only minimizes the risk of errors and miscommunications but also facilitates a more agile approach to project management.

Moreover, the integration of artificial intelligence and machine learning within digital twins opens up new horizons for predictive analytics. By harnessing vast amounts of data generated throughout the lifecycle of a building, AI algorithms can identify patterns and trends that humans might overlook. This predictive capability enables proactive maintenance, potentially extending the lifespan of structures and reducing long-term costs. It can also forecast potential issues before they become critical, ensuring a safer and more efficient construction process. In the future, we may see buildings that can essentially "think" for themselves, adjusting to environmental conditions and optimizing their performance autonomously.

Sustainability is another key area where digital twins can make a significant impact. As the construction industry increasingly prioritizes green building practices, digital twins offer a powerful tool for designing more energy-efficient structures. By simulating different scenarios and analyzing their environmental impact, architects and engineers can optimize building designs to minimize resource consumption and carbon footprints. Furthermore, digital twins can monitor a building's performance over time, suggesting adjustments to improve energy efficiency and sustainability. This holistic approach not only aligns with global efforts to combat climate change but also results in cost savings and compliance with stringent regulatory standards.

The advent of digital twins also heralds a new era of smart cities. Imagine a future where entire urban landscapes are mirrored in the digital realm, allowing city planners to simulate and optimize infrastructure before deploying it in the real world. From traffic management to public safety and utilities, digital twins can offer insights and solutions for complex urban challenges. By integrating data from various sources, such as IoT devices and social media, these digital replicas can provide a comprehensive overview of city dynamics, enabling more responsive and informed governance. This interconnectedness can lead to more resilient and adaptive urban environments, capable of evolving seamlessly with the needs of their inhabitants.

Despite the many advantages, the rise of digital twins in construction also raises important ethical considerations. Issues related to data privacy and security are paramount, given the vast amounts of information that digital twins collect and store. Ensuring that this data is protected from unauthorized access and breaches is crucial to maintaining trust in these technologies. Additionally, the automation and efficiencies brought about by digital twins may disrupt traditional job roles in the construction industry, leading to potential workforce displacement. It is essential to address these concerns through policies and initiatives that promote retraining and upskilling, ensuring that human contributions remain integral to the evolving construction sector.

In conclusion, the future possibilities of digital twins in construction are vast and transformative. From enhancing collaboration and predictive maintenance to driving sustainability and enabling smart cities, these virtual counterparts of physical structures are poised to reshape the industry. However, it is imperative that we navigate the ethical challenges they present with care, fostering a balanced integration of technology that benefits both society and the environment. As we move forward, the convergence of digital twins and construction will undoubtedly play a pivotal role in building the resilient, efficient, and intelligent structures of tomorrow.

Chapter 4
Supply Chain Management and Digital Twins.

Real-time Monitoring

In the world of supply chain management, real-time monitoring has emerged as a critical element, pivotal for maintaining efficiency and competitiveness in a fast-paced market. Digital twins, being virtual counterparts of physical entities, hold immense potential in enhancing this real-time monitoring across various levels of supply chains. Beyond just visualizing assets, digital twins provide dynamic, real-time insights by continuously assimilating data from the physical world through embedded sensors and IoT devices.

This continuous stream of data allows for unparalleled transparency, as stakeholders can continuously monitor the status and performance of assets and processes. For instance, consider a manufacturing plant where digital twins of machinery, warehouses, and even delivery vehicles are interconnected. Every piece of machinery equipped with sensors relays data about its operational parameters back to its digital twin. This enables managers to monitor performance metrics such as temperature, vibration, and energy consumption in real-time. When an anomaly is detected, such as an unexpected rise in temperature, the system can alert operators before the machinery reaches a critical failure point, thus preventing costly downtime and ensuring operational continuity.

On a broader scale, supply chains involving multiple stakeholders benefit significantly from the synchronization that digital twins offer. For example, goods in transit—whether by truck, ship, or air—often traverse international borders and involve multiple logistical entities. Digital twins of these goods, when shared across the network, allow every stakeholder to obtain instantaneous updates on the location, condition, and expected arrival time of shipments. This real-time visibility helps in optimizing routes, managing inventory levels, and ensuring that all parts of the supply chain are working in concert. Imagine a warehouse supervisor being able to see, in real-time, the precise moment when parts will arrive and thus plan labor and machine utilization more effectively.

Moreover, real-time monitoring through digital twins extends to demand forecasting and inventory management. Traditionally, supply chain management has relied on historical data and periodic reporting to estimate future demands and manage inventories. However, digital twins transform this approach by providing a real-time feedback loop. Sales data from retail outlets can flow into digital twins, allowing supply chain managers to adjust production schedules on the fly. If a particular product suddenly spikes in demand due to, say, a viral social media post, the digital twin system can detect this trend almost instantaneously and communicate the need for increased production or expedited shipping.

Real-time monitoring can also be transformative in handling disruptions. In an interconnected marketplace, disruptions can arise from various sources, such as natural disasters, political unrest, or sudden spikes in demand. Digital twins equipped with artificial intelligence and machine learning capabilities can predict potential disruptions by analyzing patterns and historical data. Once a prediction is made, the real-time monitoring system can suggest alternative routes, suppliers, or production adjustments to mitigate the impact.

Finally, the ability to monitor in real-time opens up

new horizons for sustainability in supply chain management. By analyzing data on energy usage, emissions, and waste in real-time, companies can identify inefficiencies and make real-time adjustments to minimize their ecological footprint. For example, a digital twin of a delivery vehicle can track its fuel consumption and emissions during transit and optimize the route to ensure minimal environmental impact.

In conclusion, real-time monitoring facilitated by digital twins represents a transformative shift in supply chain management, offering unprecedented transparency and agility. By enabling continuous data flow and immediate feedback, digital twins not only enhance operational efficiency and reliability but also unlock new potentials for agility, sustainability, and resilience in the face of uncertainties. As industries continue to evolve, the integration of digital twins into supply chain management is likely to become an indispensable utility, driving a new era of innovation and performance excellence.

Optimization Techniques

Optimization techniques in the realm of supply

chain management and digital twins harness the power of advanced technologies to transform traditional systems into more efficient and responsive networks. Digital twins, as faithful virtual replicas of physical assets, play a crucial role in this optimization by allowing businesses to simulate, predict, and enhance their supply chain operations in real-time.

One of the foremost ways digital twins aid in optimizing supply chains is through predictive analytics. Using real-time data and sophisticated algorithms, these virtual models can forecast potential disruptions and demand fluctuations long before they impact the physical world. For instance, a digital twin of a warehouse can predict stock shortages based on current inventory levels, supplier schedules, and historical demand patterns. This enables managers to make proactive decisions, such as adjusting orders or redistributing stock, thereby minimizing downtime and lost sales.

Furthermore, digital twins facilitate enhanced decision-making by providing a comprehensive view of the entire supply chain. By integrating data from various sources – such as transportation networks, supplier performance, and market conditions – these virtual models offer a holistic understanding of supply chain dynamics. This, in turn, enables managers to identify inefficiencies, optimize routes, and streamline operations. For example, a digital twin of a transportation network can analyze traffic patterns, vehicle performance, and fuel consumption to determine the most efficient delivery routes, ultimately reducing costs and environmental impact.

In addition to predictive capabilities, digital twins enable continuous monitoring and real-time adjustments. This dynamic approach ensures that supply chain operations remain resilient and adaptable to changing conditions. For instance, if a natural disaster disrupts a key supplier, the digital twin can quickly identify alternative sources and adjust procurement strategies accordingly. This agility not only minimizes the impact of unforeseen events but also enhances the overall reliability and robustness of the supply chain.

The integration of artificial intelligence (AI) further amplifies the optimization potential of digital twins in supply chain management. AI algorithms can analyze vast amounts of data generated by digital twins to uncover hidden patterns and insights that might be overlooked by human analysts. These insights can then inform strategies to optimize inventory levels, anticipate maintenance needs, and improve overall operational efficiency. For example, predictive maintenance enabled by AI-powered digital twins can reduce equipment downtime and extend the lifespan of critical assets, thereby ensuring a more stable and efficient supply chain.

Beyond immediate operational benefits, digital twins also facilitate long-term strategic planning. By allowing organizations to simulate various scenarios and assess the potential impact of different decisions, these virtual models enable more informed and strategic choices. Whether it's exploring the feasibility of new suppliers, evaluating the financial implications of adopting new technologies, or assessing the environmental impact of different logistical strategies, digital twins provide a safe and cost-effective environment for experimentation and analysis.

Ethical considerations also come into play when utilizing optimization techniques with digital twins.

The collection and analysis of vast amounts of data bring concerns around privacy, data security, and transparency. Organizations must ensure that their use of digital twins aligns with ethical standards and regulatory requirements, protecting sensitive information and maintaining trust with stakeholders. Additionally, the automation and efficiency gains brought by digital twins should be balanced with considerations for job displacement and the impact on the workforce.

In conclusion, digital twins represent a transformative technology for optimizing supply chain management. Through predictive analytics, real-time monitoring, AI integration, and strategic simulation, these virtual replicas enable businesses to enhance efficiency, reduce costs, and build more resilient supply chains. As the technology continues to evolve, it will undoubtedly unlock further potential and opportunities for innovation, driving the future of supply chain management to new heights of sophistication and effectiveness.

Risk Management

The integration of digital twins into supply chain management has revolutionized the way organizations predict, identify, and mitigate risks. Traditional risk management practices heavily relied on historical data and periodic assessments, which often left gaps in real-time information and adaptability. However, the adoption of digital twins has brought about a paradigm shift, enabling continuous monitoring and dynamic risk assessment.

Digital twins offer a continuous, real-time digital representation of physical assets and processes. By creating these virtual replicas, companies can simulate and analyze potential disruptions in their supply chain without waiting for them to happen. One of the most compelling applications of digital twins in risk management is their capability to predict disruptions before they manifest. Leveraging advanced analytics, machine learning, and artificial intelligence, digital twins can process vast amounts of data from various sources, including IoT sensors, historical records, and external databases. This allows for a comprehensive understanding of potential risks, ranging from machinery failures and logistical delays to environmental factors and geopolitical events.

Moreover, digital twins facilitate robust scenario planning and stress testing. Companies can simulate different risk scenarios, such as natural disasters, supplier bankruptcy, or sudden changes in market demand, to see how their supply chain would react. By doing so, they can identify vulnerabilities and develop contingency plans ahead of time. This proactive approach not only minimizes disruptions but also ensures that the supply chain remains resilient under various conditions. Additionally, these simulations help organizations prioritize their risk mitigation strategies by highlighting the most critical points of failure.

Another significant benefit of digital twins in supply chain risk management is the enhanced visibility they provide. A digital twin aggregates data from all stages of the supply chain, offering a holistic view of operations. This comprehensive visibility allows for more accurate and timely identification of potential risks. For instance, if a particular supplier's performance starts to falter, a digital twin can quickly signal the problem, allowing the company to address the issue before it escalates. This ability to detect early warning signs can prevent minor issues from becoming major disruptions.

The application of digital twins also facilitates improved collaboration and communication among stakeholders. With a shared digital representation of the supply chain, various departments and partners can access the same up-to-date information. This fosters a more cohesive approach to risk management, as all parties can quickly align and respond to potential threats. In addition, digital twins can integrate with blockchain technology to ensure data integrity and transparency, further enhancing trust and collaboration among stakeholders.

However, while digital twins offer significant advancements in risk management, they also introduce new ethical considerations. The extensive data collection required for accurate digital twin modeling raises concerns about data privacy and security. Companies must ensure that they handle and protect sensitive information appropriately, adhering to relevant regulations and ethical standards. Additionally, there is the potential for over-reliance on technology, where human judgement is undervalued. It is crucial to balance technological assistance with human expertise and decision-making to avoid blind spots and unintended consequences.

In conclusion, digital twins are transforming supply chain risk management by providing real-time, comprehensive insights and predictive capabilities. They enable proactive risk identification, robust scenario planning, and enhanced visibility, significantly bolstering supply chain resilience. However, it is essential to address accompanying ethical considerations to fully harness their potential. As these technologies continue to evolve, they promise to further revolutionize risk management practices, creating smarter, more agile supply chains capable of navigating an increasingly complex global landscape.

Integration with IoT

The integration of Digital Twins with the Internet of Things (IoT) in supply chain management represents a paradigm shift that transcends traditional methods, driving new efficiencies and insights on an unprecedented scale. In the interconnected world of IoT, where sensors and devices continuously collect and transmit data, the role of Digital Twins becomes pivotal. By creating virtual replicas of physical assets, processes, and entire systems, Digital Twins harness this ocean of data to provide real-time insights and predictive analytics, streamlining supply chain operations.

In a seamlessly connected supply chain, IoT-enabled sensors are embedded in key assets such as transportation vehicles, warehouse equipment, and individual products. These sensors generate a constant stream of data, capturing everything from temperature conditions and humidity to location tracking and operational status. Digital Twins utilize this data to create a dynamic, real-time model of the physical world, allowing supply chain managers to monitor and optimize their operations with a level of precision previously unattainable.

The convergence of IoT and Digital Twins facilitates improved visibility and control over supply chain processes. For instance, the real-time data collected by IoT devices can be fed into the Digital Twin, enabling managers to identify potential disruptions such as equipment failures or delays in transportation well before they occur. This proactive approach allows for swift corrective actions, minimizing downtime and ensuring that supply chain processes remain fluid and efficient.

Moreover, the integration of Digital Twins with IoT extends beyond reactive measures to predictive and prescriptive insights. By analyzing historical data and identifying patterns, Digital Twins can forecast future scenarios, such as demand fluctuations or potential bottlenecks in the supply chain. This predictive capability empowers managers to make informed decisions, such as adjusting inventory levels or rerouting shipments to optimize delivery times and costs.

Another transformative aspect of this integration is its impact on asset management. Through IoT sensors, managers gain unparalleled visibility into the condition and performance of their equipment and machinery. Digital Twins use this data to simulate different operating conditions, predict maintenance needs, and optimize usage schedules. This proactive maintenance approach not only extends the lifespan of assets but also significantly reduces the risk of unexpected breakdowns, thereby enhancing the overall reliability and efficiency of the supply chain.

Additionally, the synergy between Digital Twins and IoT brings about a new level of collaboration and innovation within supply chains. By providing a virtual environment where different scenarios can be tested and validated, Digital Twins enable stakeholders to experiment with new strategies and technologies without the risks associated with physical trials. This accelerates the adoption of innovations such as autonomous vehicles or advanced robotics, driving continuous improvement and competitive advantage.

However, the integration of Digital Twins with IoT also raises important ethical considerations. The vast amounts of data collected and processed come with inherent privacy and security concerns. Ensuring robust data protection measures and transparent data governance frameworks becomes essential to address these challenges. Moreover, as decision-making increasingly relies on automated insights generated by Digital Twins, it is crucial to maintain human oversight to prevent biases and ensure ethical standards are upheld.

In conclusion, the integration of Digital Twins and

IoT in supply chain management marks a transformative leap towards greater efficiency, resilience, and innovation. By leveraging real-time data and predictive analytics, this hybrid approach not only enhances operational visibility and control but also empowers supply chain managers to make informed, proactive decisions. As this technology continues to evolve, it holds the promise of reshaping the future of supply chains, unlocking new levels of performance and sustainability. However, with this power comes the responsibility to address ethical considerations, ensuring that the benefits of this technological advancement are realized in a fair and transparent manner.

Chapter 5
Advanced Analytics and Simulation.

Data Collection and Analysis

In the dynamic realm of advanced analytics and simulation, the foundational step is data collection and analysis, processes that have grown increasingly sophisticated with the advent of digital twins. At the heart of digital twins lies an unquenchable thirst for data - data that is accurate, real-time, and plentiful. The creation of a digital twin necessitates a continuous and meticulous collection of data from the physical entity it represents. Sensors, IoT devices, and other smart technologies are employed to gather vast amounts of information ranging from basic operational metrics to intricate performance parameters.

Data collection is not a mere gathering exercise; it demands precision and relevance. The sensors must be strategically placed to capture critical data points while ensuring minimal disruption to the physical object's functionality. In manufacturing, for instance, sensors might track temperature, pressure, vibration, and other environmental conditions impacting machinery. In construction, data on materials, structural integrity, and environmental factors are key. The collected data is then transmitted to a central repository where it undergoes preprocessing to remove noise and outliers, ensuring consistency and reliability.

Once data is collected, the challenge shifts to analysis. This is where advanced analytics come into play, transforming raw data into valuable insights. Machine learning algorithms and artificial intelligence are pivotal in identifying patterns, forecasting trends, and diagnosing issues. These technologies enable the digital twin to not just mimic the current state of the physical object, but also to predict future states and potential failures. Through predictive analytics, organizations can anticipate maintenance needs, optimize operations, and prevent costly downtimes.

The integration of simulation with digital twins elevates the analytical capabilities to new heights. Simulation models use the data ingested by the digital twin to create a virtual environment where various scenarios can be tested without any risk to the actual physical object. These models can replicate complex interactions and dependencies, offering a playground for engineers and analysts to experiment with different strategies and configurations. Simulations can help in understanding the impact of potential changes, from minor adjustments to significant overhauls, before any real-world implementation.

To harness the full power of simulations, the derived analytics must be cyclic and iterative. Continuous monitoring and feedback loops ensure that the digital twin remains an accurate and up-to-date representation of its physical counterpart. This iterative process facilitates ongoing refinement and improvement, fostering a deeper, actionable understanding of the physical object's behavior under diverse conditions.

Furthermore, the maze of data governance cannot be ignored in this process. Ensuring data integrity, privacy, and compliance with regulations are core to maintaining trust in the digital twin systems. Ownership and ethical considerations about data usage are paramount, especially given the sensitivity of the information often involved. Guarding against unauthorized access and ensuring that data utilization aligns with ethical standards preserves the integrity and social acceptance of these technologies.

In summary, data collection and analysis form the bedrock of digital twins and their potent simulations. It is a relentless journey of collecting accurate data, deploying advanced analytics to make sense of it, and using simulations to explore uncharted territories. The convergence of these elements unlocks unprecedented potential in optimizing operational efficiencies, enhancing predictive maintenance, and fostering innovation across various industries. As these technologies continue to evolve, the role of data will only amplify, ushering in an era where digital twins become indispensable assets in the digital transformation journey.

Simulation Models

Simulation models play a pivotal role in the creation and application of digital twins. These models are essentially the mathematical and virtual representations of real-world systems or processes, which allow for the analysis, understanding, and prediction of the behavior of physical entities. The integration of simulation models within digital twins is crucial for their functionality, as it enables users to conduct experiments and derive insights without having to interact with the actual physical objects.

Through the power of simulation models, industries can test scenarios, optimize processes, and forecast potential issues in a risk-free, cost-effective manner.

In the manufacturing sector, for instance, simulation models are employed to design and fine-tune production lines. By creating virtual replicas of machinery and workflows, engineers can simulate the entire manufacturing process, from raw material input to final product output. This allows them to identify bottlenecks, predict maintenance needs, and optimize production parameters before making any real-world changes. Consequently, production becomes more efficient, downtime is minimized, and overall costs are reduced. Moreover, simulation models enable manufacturers to swiftly adapt to changes in demand or supply chain disruptions by testing various scenarios and implementing the most effective solutions.

The construction industry also benefits significantly from the use of simulation models within digital twins. When planning a new building or infrastructure project, architects and engineers can construct a digital twin that incorporates all elements of the project, such as structural components, electrical systems, and environmental factors. By running simulations on this digital twin, they can assess the impact of different design choices, weather conditions, and material selections. This not only enhances the accuracy and reliability of project plans but also helps in forecasting potential issues that could arise during construction, thereby preventing costly delays and rework. Furthermore, simulation models support the evaluation of safety measures and the environmental sustainability of construction projects, ensuring that they meet regulatory standards and mitigate adverse impacts.

In the realm of supply chain management, simulation models are indispensable for optimizing logistics and distribution networks. Digital twins of supply chains can model the intricate web of suppliers, manufacturers, distributors, and retailers, allowing companies to visualize and analyze the flow of goods and information throughout the entire network. By simulating different supply and demand scenarios, companies can identify vulnerabilities, optimize inventory levels, and improve delivery times. This predictive capability is particularly valuable in today's dynamic and often unpredictable global market, where disruptions can arise from various sources, such as natural disasters, political instability, or pandemics. Through simulation models, businesses can develop robust contingency plans, ensure continuity of operations, and maintain a competitive edge.

The future potential of simulation models in digital twins is vast, with advancements in artificial intelligence and machine learning poised to enhance their accuracy and scope. As these technologies continue to evolve, simulation models will become more sophisticated, capable of mimicking increasingly complex systems and processes. This will facilitate the development of even more precise digital twins, enabling industries to make more informed decisions and achieve higher levels of efficiency and innovation.

However, the use of simulation models within digital twins also raises important ethical considerations. As these models become more integrated into decision-making processes, questions regarding data privacy, algorithmic bias, and the accountability of automated systems must be addressed. Ensuring that simulation models are transparent, fair, and secure will be essential for maintaining trust and fostering the responsible deployment of digital twins across various sectors.

In conclusion, simulation models form the backbone of digital twins, providing the analytical and predictive capabilities that drive their widespread adoption and effectiveness. By enabling virtual experimentation and optimization, these models offer immense benefits to industries such as manufacturing, construction, and supply chain management. As technology progresses, the potential for simulation models will continue to expand, promising even greater innovation and efficiency while necessitating careful attention to ethical implications.

Machine Learning Applications

Machine learning applications are at the heart of the advanced analytics and simulation capabilities that drive the effectiveness of digital twins. Machine learning algorithms enable digital twins to process massive amounts of data generated by their physical counterparts, thereby enhancing the predictive and prescriptive analytics capabilities of these systems. By identifying patterns and correlations within this data, machine learning can provide insights that were previously inaccessible, allowing for improved decision-making processes in various industries.

In the realm of manufacturing, machine learning algorithms are used to predict equipment failures and optimize maintenance schedules before costly downtimes occur. Using historical and real-time data, digital twins can forecast potential disruptions and suggest preventive actions based on sophisticated predictive models. This application not only enhances operational efficiency but also extends the lifespan of machinery, thus reducing overall costs.

Construction industries also leverage machine learning to predict potential project delays and manage resource allocation more effectively. By simulating different scenarios, machine learning models embedded within digital twins can provide insights into the most efficient ways to manage labor, materials, and time. This creates a more streamlined project execution process, reducing waste and improving productivity on construction sites.

Supply chain management has also seen transformative changes through the integration of machine learning with digital twins. By analyzing data from various nodes of the supply chain, these models can predict demand fluctuations, optimize inventory levels, and improve logistics planning. This ensures that products are available when and where they are needed, reducing both overstock and stockouts. The predictive capabilities of machine learning also allow for better risk management, helping companies to mitigate disruptions caused by unforeseen events such as natural disasters or geopolitical tensions.

Furthermore, the use of reinforcement learning, a subset of machine learning, within digital twins opens new frontiers in autonomous decision-making. This technique allows digital twins to learn optimal behaviors through trial and error, continuously improving their performance over time. In industries like autonomous vehicles and robotic process automation, reinforcement learning enables digital twins to navigate complex environments and make real-time decisions without human intervention.

The future potential of machine learning applications in digital twins is vast. As algorithms become more advanced and data sources more abundant, the predictive power of digital twins will continue to grow. One can envision a future where digital twins, enhanced by machine learning, can simulate entire ecosystems, from urban planning and climate modeling to personalized healthcare paths. By incorporating data from a multitude of sources, these digital twins could provide holistic solutions to some of the world's most pressing challenges.

However, the integration of machine learning with digital twins also raises ethical considerations. Issues of data privacy and security are paramount, as the volume and sensitivity of data processed by these systems increase. Additionally, there is the question of algorithmic bias, where the decision-making processes of machine learning models could perpetuate existing inequalities or create unforeseen consequences. It is crucial for organizations to adopt transparent and ethical frameworks when deploying these technologies to ensure that the benefits are equitably distributed.

In conclusion, the synergy between machine learning and digital twins holds immense promise for revolutionizing industries through advanced analytics and simulation. By harnessing the power of machine learning, digital twins can provide deeper insights, optimize operations, and predict future outcomes with unprecedented accuracy. As we continue to explore and expand the capabilities of these technologies, it is essential to address the ethical implications to foster a future where digital innovation serves the greater good.

Decision Support Systems

Decision Support Systems (DSS) have evolved tremendously with the advent of digital twins and advanced analytics, transforming the way industries handle complex decision-making processes. At their core, DSS are computer-based systems designed to assist in the decision-making activities of an organization by collecting, processing, and presenting relevant information. With the integration of digital twins, these systems now offer a more robust and dynamic framework, enabling real-time insights and simulations that were once unimaginable.

Digital twins act as the backbone of modern DSS by providing a virtual environment that mirrors physical assets, systems, or processes. This capability allows stakeholders to monitor, analyze, and predict performance without the constraints of the physical world. For instance, in manufacturing, digital twins can simulate the production line to forecast potential bottlenecks, equipment failures, or quality issues. These simulations are driven by data collected from sensors attached to physical assets, continuously feeding the digital counterpart with real-time information. By leveraging advanced analytics, historical data, and machine learning algorithms, DSS can then generate actionable insights, helping decision-makers to optimize operations, reduce downtime, and enhance efficiency.

One remarkable advantage of digital twins in DSS is their ability to conduct what-if scenarios. These scenarios are crucial for testing various strategies or changes in a controlled virtual environment before implementing them in the real world. In the construction industry, for example, digital twins can be used to explore different design options, assess the impact of changes in materials, and even simulate the construction process to identify potential issues before they occur. This proactive approach significantly reduces risks, saves costs, and ensures better adherence to project timelines.

Moreover, digital twins enhance the predictive capabilities of DSS through continuous learning and adaptation. As these digital replicas accumulate more data over time, their simulations and analyses become more accurate and reliable. This continuous improvement loop is vital in industries where conditions change frequently and unpredictably. In supply chain management, for example, digital twins can predict disruptions caused by factors such as weather changes, geopolitical events, or fluctuations in demand. By simulating different scenarios and their potential impacts, DSS can provide recommendations for mitigating risks and ensuring smooth operations.

The integration of advanced analytics and digital twins also enhances collaboration across different departments and stakeholders. A centralized digital twin can serve as a single source of truth, where all relevant data and insights are accessible to various users in real-time. This transparency facilitates better communication, faster decision-making, and more aligned strategies. In a logistics company, for instance, digital twins can help synchronize activities between suppliers, carriers, and customers, ensuring that everyone has access to the same up-to-date information and can make informed decisions promptly.

However, the rise of digital twins and advanced analytics in DSS also brings ethical considerations to the forefront. The vast amount of data collected and analyzed raises concerns about privacy and security. Organizations must ensure that they are handling data responsibly, complying with regulations, and implementing robust cybersecurity measures to protect sensitive information. Moreover, the reliance on automated decision-making processes prompts questions about accountability and the potential for bias in algorithm-driven insights. It is crucial for organizations to maintain a human-in-the-loop approach where expert judgment complements automated recommendations, ensuring that ethical standards are upheld.

In conclusion, the integration of digital twins with advanced analytics is revolutionizing Decision Support Systems by providing real-time, data-driven insights and predictive capabilities that enhance decision-making processes across various industries. While the benefits are immense, it is equally important to address the ethical and security challenges that arise, fostering responsible and transparent use of these technologies. This evolution represents a significant leap towards more efficient, informed, and proactive decision-making in the digital age.

Chapter 6
Technological Infrastructure.

Cloud Computing

The rise of digital twins and virtual assets owes much of its feasibility and efficiency to the advancement of cloud computing. At its core, cloud computing serves as the backbone, providing the necessary computational power, storage, and versatility required by these sophisticated digital models. The synergy between cloud computing and digital twins is nothing short of revolutionary, enabling a seamless integration of vast amounts of data and real-time processing capabilities that were previously unimaginable.

Cloud computing has democratized access to high-performance computing resources, eliminating the need for organizations to invest heavily in physical infrastructure. By leveraging cloud services, businesses can store, process, and analyze extensive datasets generated by digital twins without the constraints of legacy systems. This scalability is crucial, as the complexity and size of data involved in monitoring and simulating physical assets can be overwhelming. The cloud's capacity to dynamically scale resources ensures that businesses can handle peak loads and complex simulations efficiently.

In addition to scalability, cloud computing offers unparalleled accessibility. Digital twin technology thrives on real-time data and continuous monitoring, which necessitates a robust and easily accessible platform. Through the cloud, data can be ingested from a multitude of sources, including IoT sensors, enterprise systems, and user inputs, ensuring a comprehensive and up-to-date virtual representation of physical assets. This connectivity is not limited by geographic boundaries, enabling global collaboration and information sharing across various stakeholders and industries.

Moreover, cloud computing enhances the ability to integrate advanced analytical tools and machine learning algorithms into digital twin ecosystems. Modern clouds are equipped with sophisticated AI and big data analytics capabilities, allowing for the automation of data processing, anomaly detection, and predictive maintenance. This integration is pivotal for extracting actionable insights from the massive datasets that digital twins generate. By utilizing these advanced tools, businesses can anticipate potential issues before they arise, optimize operational efficiencies, and make informed strategic decisions.

One of the transformative aspects of cloud computing in the realm of digital twins is the facilitation of a centralized data repository. In traditional systems, data often resides in silos, making it difficult to achieve a holistic view of asset performance. The cloud breaks down these barriers, aggregating data into a single, unified platform. This not only streamlines workflows but also enables more accurate simulations and analyses, as the digital twin can draw from a comprehensive dataset encompassing all aspects of the physical counterpart.

Security and data privacy are paramount considerations in the deployment of digital twins, and cloud providers have made significant strides in enhancing these aspects. Advanced encryption methods, secure access controls, and rigorous compliance standards are now integral to cloud services, addressing the concerns of data breaches and unauthorized access. With these robust security measures, organizations can confidently leverage cloud-based digital twins without compromising sensitive information.

Ultimately, the fusion of cloud computing and digital twins represents a paradigm shift in how industries manage and optimize their resources. By harnessing the extraordinary capabilities of the cloud, businesses can build resilient, data-driven infrastructures that transcend traditional limitations. The predictive power, operational efficiency, and collaborative potential offered by this combination not only revolutionize current practices but also pave the way for future innovations. In this intertwined relationship, cloud computing is not just a tool but a fundamental enabler that propels the digital twin technology into a new era of operational excellence and strategic foresight.

Edge Computing

Edge computing is emerging as a cornerstone in the technological infrastructure essential for the rise of digital twins and virtual assets. Unlike traditional cloud computing, which centralizes data processing in remote data centers, edge computing decentralizes data processing by bringing it closer to the devices that generate the data. This shift is crucial for various industries, including manufacturing, construction, and supply chain management, as it enhances real-time decision-making capabilities, reduces latency, and improves the efficiency of data handling.

In manufacturing, the implementation of digital twins necessitates the rapid processing of vast amounts of data generated by sensors and machinery. Edge computing enables manufacturing facilities to process this data in real-time at the source, thus allowing for immediate adjustments to be made to operations. For example, if a sensor on a production line detects an anomaly, an edge computing system can analyze the data locally and prompt corrective measures instantly, thereby minimizing downtime and maintaining the continuity of production. This immediate response time is crucial for maintaining the high levels of efficiency and quality control that modern manufacturing demands.

The construction industry also benefits significantly from edge computing, particularly in the context of creating and maintaining digital twins of construction sites. Construction sites are dynamic environments where conditions can change rapidly, and real-time data processing is critical. Edge computing allows for the local analysis of data from various sensors deployed on a construction site, such as those monitoring structural integrity, environmental conditions, and machinery performance. By processing this data at the edge, construction managers can receive actionable insights in real-time, enabling them to make informed decisions that enhance safety, optimize resource allocation, and ensure the project adheres to timelines. The immediacy of data processing also facilitates better coordination among the workforce, machinery, and materials on-site, which is essential for the efficient progress of construction projects.

In supply chain management, the role of edge computing is equally transformative. As goods move through various stages of the supply chain, they generate substantial amounts of data regarding their location, condition, and handling. To maintain the integrity and efficiency of the supply chain, it is critical to process this data as close to its source as possible. Edge computing allows for this by enabling the local analysis of data generated by IoT devices and sensors attached to shipments, warehouses, and transportation vehicles. This local data processing helps in real-time tracking of goods, immediate detection of any issues such as temperature deviations or unauthorized access, and prompt decision-making to reroute or protect shipments. The result is a more resilient and transparent supply chain that can adapt quickly to disturbances and meet the demand for just-in-time inventory management.

Looking ahead, the future potential of edge computing in supporting digital twins and virtual assets is expansive. As the number and capability of connected devices grow, the amount of data generated will multiply exponentially. Edge computing can efficiently manage this data deluge by distributing computational power throughout the network, thereby alleviating the burden on central servers and reducing the risk of network congestion. Furthermore, edge computing enhances the security of data by minimizing the need for data to travel over potentially vulnerable networks, thereby reducing the risk of cyber-attacks. Ethical considerations such as data privacy and autonomy in decision-making also find a supportive framework in edge computing, as much of the data processing remains localized and within the control of the owner.

In conclusion, edge computing is not just an optional enhancement but a vital component of the technological infrastructure that drives the effectiveness and future development of digital twins and virtual assets. It brings the processing power closer to the data sources, facilitating real-time analysis, reducing latency, and supporting immediate and informed decision-making across various industries. Through its integration, edge computing provides the backbone needed for the seamless and efficient functioning of digital twins, ushering in an era where data-driven innovation can thrive at unprecedented speeds.

Networking Requirements

The successful implementation of digital twins and virtual assets hinges significantly on robust networking requirements. The unique nature of these technologies, which involve the creation and synchronization of real-time virtual replicas of physical assets, demands exceptional connectivity, data transfer capabilities, and network resilience.

Central to the foundation of digital twins is the need

for high-speed, low-latency networks. The real-time data transmission required to maintain accurate virtual representations necessitates a broad bandwidth and minimal latency to ensure there is no perceptible delay between changes in the physical world and their reflection in the digital twin. This is particularly critical in industries such as manufacturing and construction, where even minor delays can result in discrepancies that could affect performance, efficiency, or safety. Consequently, the roll-out of 5G networks is poised to play a pivotal role, providing the requisite speed and reliability that older network technologies may struggle to deliver.

Moreover, the vast amounts of data generated by sensors, IoT devices, and edge computing components need to be effectively managed and transmitted. This necessitates not only excellent connectivity but also advanced network management capabilities. Network slicing, a feature enabled by 5G, can be particularly beneficial as it allows the creation of virtual networks with dedicated resources tailored to specific applications and requirements of digital twins. This ensures that crucial data streams related to operational integrity can be prioritized and safeguarded against congestion or failures in other parts of the network.

Security is another paramount consideration in the networking infrastructure for digital twins and virtual assets. The sheer volume of data being transmitted and the critical nature of many of these applications make them potential targets for cyber-attacks. Thus, secure and resilient networks are imperative. This involves deploying robust encryption protocols, secure authentication methods, and continuous monitoring for potential threats. Furthermore, creating a segmented and well-structured network architecture can help isolate and protect sensitive data, reducing the risk of widespread breaches.

On top of this, the interoperability of networks is crucial. Digital twins often involve multiple stakeholders, platforms, and systems, each with its own set of requirements and standards. Ensuring that these disparate systems can communicate effectively necessitates the use of standardized protocols and open architectures. This promotes seamless data exchange and integration, allowing digital twins to function optimally across different devices and environments.

Another aspect that cannot be overlooked is the scalability of networking solutions. As the adoption of digital twins expands and their applications proliferate, the demand for network resources will inevitably grow. Thus, the networking infrastructure must be capable of scaling up to handle increased data loads without compromising performance or reliability. This includes not only physical infrastructure but also software-defined networking (SDN) solutions that provide the flexibility to manage and optimize network resources dynamically.

In addition to data transmission, the role of cloud computing and edge computing in supporting digital twins is also significant. Cloud platforms offer the storage capacity and processing power required to handle and analyze the extensive datasets generated. Meanwhile, edge computing brings computational capabilities closer to the data source, reducing latency and enhancing real-time data processing abilities. The synergy between cloud and edge computing, facilitated by a robust and adaptive networking framework, is central to the efficient operation of digital twins.

In summary, the networking requirements for digital twins and virtual assets are multifaceted, encompassing speed, reliability, security, interoperability, scalability, and an effective integration of cloud and edge computing. As these technologies continue to evolve and integrate deeper into various industries, understanding and addressing these networking requirements will be crucial to unlocking their full potential and ensuring their seamless and secure operation.

Data Security

Data security is a cornerstone in the technological infrastructure supporting digital twins and virtual assets. As these technologies become more integral to modern industry and our everyday lives, ensuring that the sensitive data they generate, store, and process remains protected is paramount. At its core, data security involves safeguarding information from unauthorized access, corruption, or theft throughout its lifecycle. In the context of digital twins, this challenge is amplified due to the vast amounts of complex data involved and the interconnected nature of the systems.

A digital twin is intricately intertwined with its physical counterpart, constantly collecting and updating information in real-time. This continuous flow of data includes everything from routine operational metrics to critical and sensitive information about the physical object's performance and status. Protecting this data requires a multi-faceted approach encompassing robust encryption methods, secure communication channels, and stringent access controls. Encryption ensures that data remains inaccessible to unauthorized users during transmission and storage, transforming it into unreadable ciphertext. This is particularly crucial when data travels across potentially insecure networks or is stored in cloud-based systems vulnerable to breaches.

Communications between the physical object and its digital twin must also be fortified. Secure communication channels, such as Virtual Private Networks (VPNs) and Transport Layer Security (TLS), play an essential role in ensuring that data is transmitted safely without interception by malicious entities. Furthermore, employing advanced authentication techniques like multi-factor authentication (MFA) adds an additional layer of defense, verifying the identities of all parties interacting with the digital twin system before granting access.

However, technological measures alone are not sufficient. The human element of data security cannot be overlooked. As employees interact with digital twins and virtual assets, they become potential vectors for security breaches, whether through negligence or malicious intent. As such, regular training and awareness programs for staff are critical, ensuring they understand the importance of data security and are equipped with best practices to mitigate risks. This includes recognizing phishing attempts, adhering to secure password practices, and understanding the critical nature of their role in the security framework.

Moreover, the data lifecycle within the context of digital twins includes stages that require vigilant oversight. From data creation and acquisition to storage, usage, sharing, and disposal, each phase presents unique security challenges and requires specific protective measures. Data governance strategies must be instituted to define how data should be handled, who has access to it, and how it should be protected at each stage. This ensures consistency and adherence to regulatory standards such as GDPR or HIPAA, which may impose legal obligations regarding data privacy and protection.

As digital twins become more complex and ubiquitous, they also become more attractive targets for cybercriminals. These systems often serve as critical nodes in broader industrial Internet of Things (IoT) networks, and a breach in one part of the system can potentially compromise vast swathes of the network. Consequently, in addition to preventive measures, robust incident response plans must also be in place. These plans enable rapid detection, containment, and remediation of security incidents, minimizing potential damage and ensuring quick recovery of operations.

The future potential of digital twins and virtual assets is limitless, ushering in an era where our physical and virtual worlds are seamlessly integrated. Yet, this vision is contingent on robust data security frameworks. Only through a comprehensive approach that blends technological defenses with vigilant governance and human awareness can we fully realize the benefits of these innovations while safeguarding against the multifaceted risks they bring. Ensuring data security is not a one-time task but a continuous commitment to adapting and evolving with emerging threats in the digital landscape.

Chapter 7
Ethical and Privacy Considerations.

Data Ownership

Data ownership is a critical aspect when discussing the ethical and privacy considerations surrounding digital twins and virtual assets. As digital replicas of physical objects, digital twins often involve the collection, storage, and processing of vast amounts of data. This data can include sensitive information about the operations, configurations, and even the behavior of physical assets. The question of who owns this data, therefore, becomes central to the ethical discourse.

When an organization creates a digital twin, it typically generates and collects data from the physical object it is replicating. For instance, in manufacturing, sensors embedded in machinery capture data that is then used to update the digital twin. However, this raises an immediate question: Does the organization own the data generated by these sensors, or does the ownership lie with the manufacturer of the sensors or the machinery? This question does not have a straightforward answer and can be further complicated when third parties are involved in data processing or storage.

Data ownership becomes even murkier when considering shared or collaborative environments. In supply chain management, multiple stakeholders, including suppliers, distributors, and retailers, might access and contribute data to a digital twin. Each entity might believe that it holds ownership rights over the data it contributes, leading to potential conflicts. The need for clear contractual agreements and guidelines on data ownership and usage rights is crucial to avoid disputes and ensure transparency.

Moreover, the rights and responsibilities concerning data ownership are not just about claiming possession but also about the ethical use of that data. Data ownership should guarantee certain privileges, such as control over data dissemination, the ability to monetize data, and the right to erase data if necessary. At the same time, data owners should be held accountable for ensuring data privacy, securing against unauthorized access, and maintaining data integrity. Balancing these rights and responsibilities is challenging and necessitates robust legal frameworks.

Another layer of complexity in data ownership is the

potential for personal data to be intertwined with the operational data of digital twins. For example, smart buildings equipped with digital twins may gather data not only about the building's structural health but also about the movement and behavior of its occupants. In such cases, it is imperative to distinguish between operational data, which pertains to the building's functionalities, and personal data, which involves privacy considerations for individuals. Ensuring that personal data is anonymized and that individuals' privacy rights are respected should be a priority for any entity claiming ownership over the data.

The issue of data ownership also extends to the evolving landscape of data sovereignty, wherein data ownership and control may be influenced by national or international regulations. Different countries have varying laws and regulations concerning data protection, and organizations must navigate these regulations to ensure compliance. This aspect becomes particularly relevant in cross-border operations where digital twins and virtual assets are used across multiple jurisdictions.

In conclusion, data ownership in the realm of digital

twins and virtual assets is a multifaceted issue involving ethical, legal, and operational considerations. Defining clear ownership rights and responsibilities, ensuring transparency in data usage, respecting privacy, and complying with regulatory requirements are essential steps to address the ethical implications surrounding this technology. As digital twins become more integral to various industries, the dialogue on data ownership will undoubtedly continue to evolve, necessitating ongoing attention and adaptation.

Privacy Concerns

As we delve into the domain of digital twins and virtual assets, one cannot overlook the significant privacy concerns that accompany the proliferation of these technologies. Digital twins, by their very nature, generate and rely on vast amounts of data. This data often encompasses detailed information about the physical objects they replicate, as well as the environments in which these objects operate. Consequently, the collection, storage, and utilization of such data raise profound concerns about privacy and data security.

One of the foremost privacy challenges is the sheer

volume and granularity of data required to create and maintain digital twins. These virtual replicas necessitate continuous data streams to ensure they accurately reflect their physical counterparts. In sectors such as manufacturing, this data could include specifics about machinery performance, maintenance schedules, and even the operational habits of employees. In construction, it might entail detailed architectural plans, safety protocols, and site activity logs. The extensive data collection required for these virtual models can inadvertently expose sensitive information, making it crucial to implement stringent data protection measures.

Moreover, the interconnectivity of digital twins means that data from various sources is often pooled together to create a comprehensive virtual representation. This amalgamation of data compounds the risk of privacy breaches, as it increases the chances of sensitive information being inadvertently shared or exposed. For instance, a digital twin in supply chain management might integrate data from multiple stakeholders, ranging from manufacturers to logistics providers, all of whom have varying levels of data security protocols. Any weak link in this chain could potentially compromise the privacy of the entire dataset.

Another critical issue is the potential misuse of data. While digital twins can offer unparalleled insights and drive efficiencies, the detailed data they generate can also be exploited for purposes beyond their intended use. For example, data pertaining to employee behavior captured by digital twins in a factory setting could be misused for surveillance or intrusive performance monitoring, infringing on worker privacy. Likewise, in the construction industry, detailed site data might be inappropriately accessed and used to inform competitive bidding strategies, resulting in unfair market advantages.

The regulatory landscape surrounding data privacy adds another layer of complexity. Different jurisdictions have varying regulations concerning data protection, such as the General Data Protection Regulation (GDPR) in the European Union or the California Consumer Privacy Act (CCPA) in the United States. Organizations leveraging digital twins must navigate this intricate regulatory environment meticulously to ensure compliance when handling and processing data. Failure to adhere to these regulations can result not only in hefty fines but also in significant reputational damage.

Furthermore, the ethical considerations surrounding the consent of data subjects cannot be ignored. For personal data to be incorporated into digital twins responsibly, explicit consent must be obtained from the individuals involved. This is especially pertinent in environments where digital twins are used to monitor personal activities or behavioral patterns. Ensuring that individuals are fully informed about how their data will be used and that they provide genuine consent is fundamental to addressing privacy concerns.

In conclusion, while digital twins and virtual assets promise transformative benefits across various industries, they also bring to the fore substantial privacy challenges. To harness the potential of these technologies responsibly, it is imperative to prioritize robust data security measures, navigate the diverse regulatory landscape diligently, and uphold the highest ethical standards in data usage. By addressing these privacy concerns proactively, we can pave the way for the responsible and ethical deployment of digital twins, ensuring that the benefits are realized without compromising the privacy and trust of individuals and organizations.

Ethical Frameworks

As we delve into the ethical frameworks surrounding digital twins and virtual assets, it is imperative to recognize that these technologies, while immensely beneficial, are not without their ethical challenges. The implementation of digital twins—the virtual replicas of physical objects—presents a myriad of ethical considerations that extend beyond their technological capabilities. Ethical frameworks serve as the guiding principles that ensure the responsible and fair use of these technologies, addressing concerns ranging from data privacy to the potential impact on employment and societal structures.

One of the primary ethical concerns with digital twins is the issue of data privacy. Digital twins thrive on data; their accuracy and usefulness are directly proportional to the amount and quality of data they receive. However, this data, often collected in real-time from physical objects, may include sensitive information. For instance, in a healthcare context, a digital twin of a patient could provide invaluable insights for treatment plans but also raise significant privacy issues. The collection, storage, and use of personal health data must adhere to stringent privacy regulations such as the General Data Protection Regulation (GDPR) in Europe and the Health Insurance Portability and Accountability Act (HIPAA) in the United States. Upholding these regulations within ethical frameworks ensures that individuals' privacy rights are preserved despite the technological advancements.

Furthermore, ethical frameworks must address the potential for digital twins to exacerbate inequalities. While digital twins could revolutionize industries by enhancing efficiency and enabling predictive maintenance, their benefits might not be uniformly distributed. Organizations with significant resources are more likely to leverage these technologies effectively, potentially widening the gap between large corporations and smaller enterprises. An ethical framework must consider fair access and strive to create policies that encourage equitable distribution of the benefits derived from digital twins.

This involves providing support and resources to smaller entities to adopt these technologies, thereby fostering inclusiveness and preventing the deepening of socioeconomic divides.

In addition to concerns of fairness and privacy, ethical frameworks need to contemplate the impact of digital twins on employment. As industries increasingly incorporate digital twins, certain job roles may become obsolete, replaced by automated systems and predictive analytics. This technological displacement poses ethical questions about the future of work and the social responsibility of corporations. Ethical guidelines should encourage companies to invest in employee retraining and upskilling programs to mitigate the potential adverse effects on employment. By focusing on human-centric approaches, these frameworks can ensure a more socially responsible integration of digital twins into the workforce.

Moreover, there is a pressing need to address the ethical implications of decision-making by AI-driven digital twins. These virtual replicas often rely on sophisticated algorithms and artificial intelligence to make decisions or provide recommendations.

Transparency and accountability in these processes are critical. Ethical frameworks should mandate that the algorithms used in digital twins are explainable and auditable. This ensures that decisions made by these systems can be traced and understood, thereby fostering trust and accountability. Additionally, these frameworks must consider the potential biases in algorithms which could lead to unfair or discriminatory outcomes. Regular audits and ethical reviews of these algorithms are necessary to ensure they operate fairly and impartially.

In summary, the ethical frameworks for digital twins and virtual assets must be comprehensive and multi-faceted, addressing concerns of data privacy, equity, employment, and decision-making. As these technologies continue to evolve, it is crucial that ethical considerations remain at the forefront, guiding their development and deployment in ways that are socially responsible, transparent, and equitable. Only by doing so can we fully harness the potential of digital twins while safeguarding the values that uphold our societal well-being.

Regulations and Compliance

In navigating the rapidly evolving landscape of digital twins and virtual assets, understanding the regulatory and compliance framework is essential for ensuring ethical and privacy considerations are adequately addressed. As these technologies permeate various industries, the need for comprehensive regulations becomes paramount to address concerns related to data security, privacy, and the broader ethical implications of their deployment.

One of the primary regulatory challenges with digital twins is the vast amount of data they generate and utilize. Digital twins rely on real-time data collection from physical counterparts, often involving sensitive information. This necessitates stringent data protection measures to prevent unauthorized access and misuse. Regulatory frameworks like the General Data Protection Regulation (GDPR) in Europe set rigorous standards for data privacy and security, requiring organizations to implement robust data protection protocols. Compliance with such regulations ensures that companies handling digital twins prioritize individual privacy rights and mitigate risks associated with data breaches.

Moreover, the cross-border nature of digital twins adds another layer of complexity to regulatory compliance. Data used by digital twins often flows across international borders, making it subject to varying legal standards. Organizations must navigate this intricate web of regulations to ensure compliance in all jurisdictions where they operate. This requires a deep understanding of local data protection laws and international agreements, such as the EU-U.S. Privacy Shield framework, which governs transatlantic exchanges of personal data for commercial purposes. Adhering to these regulations is crucial for maintaining trust and avoiding hefty penalties associated with non-compliance.

Ethical considerations also play a significant role in the regulatory landscape of digital twins. As these technologies enable unprecedented levels of monitoring and control, questions arise regarding the ethical boundaries of such capabilities. For instance, in industries like healthcare, digital twins of patients could revolutionize personalized medicine but also risk infringing on patient privacy. Regulatory bodies must establish clear guidelines that balance innovation with ethical considerations, ensuring that the use of digital twins does not compromise individual rights or lead to discriminatory practices.

The rapid pace of technological advancement often outstrips the development of corresponding regulatory frameworks, leading to a reactive rather than proactive approach to regulation. To address this gap, some governments and industry bodies advocate for the creation of sandbox environments where digital twin technologies can be tested within a controlled regulatory context. These sandboxes enable innovators to experiment and refine their technologies while working closely with regulators to identify potential issues and develop appropriate compliance strategies. Such collaborative efforts are essential for creating a regulatory environment that fosters innovation while safeguarding ethical and privacy standards.

Furthermore, transparency and accountability are key components of an effective regulatory framework for digital twins. Organizations must be transparent about their data practices, including how data is collected, processed, and utilized in creating and maintaining digital twins. Regulatory bodies should enforce stringent disclosure requirements that compel companies to provide clear and accessible information to stakeholders, including consumers, about their data practices. This transparency not only builds trust but also empowers individuals to make informed decisions about their engagement with digital twin technologies.

In conclusion, regulations and compliance play a critical role in addressing the ethical and privacy considerations associated with digital twins and virtual assets. As these technologies continue to evolve and integrate into various sectors, a robust regulatory framework is essential to ensure data security, respect individual privacy, and uphold ethical standards. By adopting a proactive, collaborative approach to regulation, stakeholders can create an environment where innovation thrives while safeguarding the rights and interests of individuals and society at large.

Chapter 8
Future Trends and Opportunities.

Integration with AI

As digital twins and virtual assets gain traction across various industries, their integration with artificial intelligence (AI) emerges as a transformative trend. The symbiotic relationship between these technologies promises to unlock unprecedented levels of innovation and efficiency. When digital twins are enhanced with AI, they become more than just static replicas; they evolve into dynamic, intelligent entities capable of learning, predicting, and optimizing in real-time.

The fusion of AI with digital twins starts with data. Digital twins generate vast amounts of data, mirroring every detail and process of their physical counterparts. AI algorithms, particularly those focused on machine learning, thrive on large datasets. They can analyze this data to identify patterns and correlations that would be invisible to the human eye. In manufacturing, for example, an AI-enhanced digital twin can predict equipment failures by analyzing sensor data to detect early signs of wear and tear. This predictive capability allows for timely maintenance, reducing downtime and saving costs.

Moreover, AI integration brings a level of adaptability to digital twins that is crucial for industries characterized by constant change and complexity. In construction, digital twins equipped with AI can simulate various scenarios, such as different weather conditions or supply chain disruptions, to optimize project planning and resource allocation. By learning from each iteration and outcome, these digital twins continuously improve their models and predictions, making them invaluable tools for decision-makers.

The realm of supply chain management also benefits immensely from this integration. AI can process and analyze the data generated by digital twins across the entire supply chain, from raw material extraction to product delivery. It can optimize routes, predict demand fluctuations, and even mitigate risks by identifying potential bottlenecks or disruptions before they occur. This level of insight and foresight is pivotal in today's global market, where supply chain resilience has become a top priority.

In addition to operational efficiencies, AI-enhanced

digital twins open up new frontiers in innovation and product development. By combining historical data with real-time inputs, AI can help digital twins simulate and test new designs or processes virtually. This reduces the time and cost associated with physical prototyping and accelerates the innovation cycle. Companies can experiment with multiple variables and quickly identify the best solutions, leading to faster, more efficient product development.

Furthermore, the integration of AI with digital twins fosters a deeper understanding of system behaviors and interactions. In smart cities, for instance, digital twins of infrastructure can work with AI systems to manage energy consumption, traffic flow, and emergency response dynamically. These intelligent systems can make real-time adjustments based on an array of data inputs, enhancing urban efficiency and sustainability.

However, the burgeoning integration of AI with digital twins also raises important ethical and governance considerations. The reliance on vast amounts of data necessitates stringent data privacy and security measures. Moreover, the decision-making capabilities of AI must be transparent and accountable to ensure fairness and avoid biases. As these technologies continue to evolve, developing robust frameworks for ethical AI usage within digital twins becomes paramount.

The integration of AI with digital twins is not merely an enhancement but a fundamental evolution. It transforms digital replicas from passive models into active, intelligent systems capable of reshaping industries and driving future innovation. By harnessing the power of AI, digital twins can unlock new levels of efficiency, adaptability, and insight, paving the way for a more intelligent and interconnected world. As we venture deeper into this era of digital transformation, the journey of digital twins and AI integration is only just beginning, and its potential is boundless.

Smart Cities

The advent of digital twins is set to revolutionize not only individual industries but entire urban ecosystems. Smart cities, defined by their integration of information and communication technologies to enhance the quality and performance of urban services, stand to benefit enormously from digital twin technology. At the heart of future urban environments, digital twins promise to transform cities into smarter, more efficient, and more sustainable habitats for their inhabitants.

In smart cities, digital twins serve as dynamic virtual replicas of physical environments that encompass buildings, infrastructure, transportation systems, and even entire districts. These digital counterparts are continuously updated with real-time data captured by an array of sensors and IoT devices embedded throughout the urban landscape. The continuous flow of data enables city planners and administrators to monitor, simulate, and optimize various aspects of urban living with unprecedented precision and speed.

One of the most promising applications of digital twins in smart cities is in optimizing traffic management and transportation systems. By creating a virtual replica of the city's road network and integrating data from traffic cameras, GPS devices, and public transit systems, city officials can gain a comprehensive understanding of traffic flow and congestion points. With this knowledge, they can devise and implement strategies to alleviate traffic congestion, reduce travel times, and minimize carbon emissions. For instance, dynamic traffic light control systems can be fine-tuned in real time to respond to changing traffic patterns, enhancing both efficiency and safety.

Another area where digital twin technology can have a significant impact is in the management of urban infrastructure. Cities worldwide face the challenges of aging infrastructure and the need for sustainable growth. Digital twins of bridges, tunnels, water systems, and power grids allow for continuous monitoring and predictive maintenance. By analyzing data from sensors embedded in these structures, city engineers can predict potential failures and schedule timely maintenance, thereby reducing downtime and preventing catastrophic incidents. This proactive approach not only saves costs but also enhances the reliability and resilience of urban infrastructure.

Energy management is yet another domain where smart cities can harness the power of digital twins. Through the creation of digital replicas of entire energy grids, cities can monitor and optimize energy distribution and consumption patterns. Renewable energy sources, such as solar panels and wind turbines, can be seamlessly integrated into the energy grid with the help of digital twins, ensuring an efficient and balanced supply of energy. Moreover, digital twins can facilitate the implementation of smart grids, where energy usage in buildings can be optimized based on real-time demand, leading to significant energy savings and a reduced environmental footprint.

The concept of digital twins extends beyond infrastructure to encompass the built environment as well. Digital replicas of buildings enable urban planners to simulate various scenarios related to sustainability, energy efficiency, and occupant comfort. For instance, simulations can predict the impact of different architectural designs on natural light and ventilation, allowing architects to create buildings that maximize energy efficiency and occupant well-being. Furthermore, digital twins can facilitate the integration of smart building technologies, such as automated lighting, heating, and cooling systems, which can be adjusted based on real-time data to enhance comfort while minimizing energy use.

While the potential of digital twins in smart cities is immense, it also raises important ethical considerations. Issues related to data privacy, security, and governance must be addressed to ensure that the benefits of these technologies are realized without compromising individual rights and freedoms. Transparent policies and robust cybersecurity measures must be implemented to safeguard sensitive data and protect against cyber threats.

In conclusion, the integration of digital twin technology in smart cities promises to create urban environments that are more efficient, sustainable, and responsive to the needs of their inhabitants. By leveraging real-time data, cities can optimize their infrastructure, transportation systems, and energy usage, ultimately enhancing the quality of life for their residents. However, the ethical implications of these advancements must be carefully navigated to ensure a balanced and equitable urban future.

Healthcare Innovations

In the realm of healthcare, digital twins are on the brink of revolutionizing patient care, medical procedures, and overall health management. Digital twins, virtual replicas of physical entities, hold the potential to remodel healthcare delivery through unparalleled precision and personalized treatment plans. As the healthcare industry continues to evolve, increasingly pressing demands for efficiency, accuracy, and tailored medical interventions are becoming more prominent. Digital twins, by replicating physiological and anatomical details, are offering monumental advancements that promise to meet these challenges head-on.

A digital twin of a patient, created from detailed imaging, genetic data, and continuous health monitoring, can provide a comprehensive view of an individual's health status. This virtual model allows healthcare professionals to predict the onset of diseases, customise treatment plans, and monitor the progression of illnesses in real-time. By simulating various scenarios, such as the impact of a specific drug or surgical procedure on the patient's unique physiology, medical professionals can make more informed decisions, reducing risks and improving outcomes. This leap in predictive medicine ensures that treatments are not only timely but also precisely targeted, thereby reducing the incidence of adverse reactions and optimizing therapeutic efficacy.

Moreover, the advent of digital twins facilitates unprecedented advancements in personalized healthcare. Genomic data, combined with lifestyle and environmental factors, can be used to build a digital twin that mirrors the patient's current health status. This dynamic model can then be employed to predict how an individual might respond to various treatments, allowing for medical interventions that are tailored to the precise needs of the patient. Such personalized approaches herald a shift from the traditional, often one-size-fits-all methodology, to more bespoke medical care. In chronic disease management, for example, digital twins can empower patients with diabetes or cardiovascular diseases to manage their conditions more effectively by providing continuous feedback and actionable insights.

The impact of digital twins extends to surgical procedures as well. Surgeons can now rehearse complex operations on digital models before making an incision on the actual patient, thereby enhancing precision and reducing the likelihood of complications. This ability to plan and simulate surgeries could potentially transform surgical training and education by providing a risk-free environment where practitioners can hone their skills. Additionally, post-surgery, digital twins can help in monitoring recovery and predicting potential post-operative complications, ensuring timely medical interventions if necessary.

Ethical considerations, however, must not be overlooked. The creation and use of digital twins involve sensitive health data, raising concerns regarding data privacy and security. Safeguarding this information is crucial to maintaining patient trust and complying with regulatory standards. Furthermore, the integration of digital twins into the healthcare system requires careful navigation of ethical landscapes, particularly concerning consent, data ownership, and the potential implications of predictive analytics on patient anxiety and the psychological burden of predicted illnesses.

Looking forward, the incorporation of artificial intelligence and machine learning with digital twins is expected to enhance their predictive accuracy and functionality. These technologies can sift through massive datasets, recognizing patterns and correlations that human eyes might miss, thereby refining the fidelity of digital twins. As digital twins continue to evolve, they are poised to become an integral part of preventive medicine, potentially enabling earlier detection of diseases and more effective interventions.

In conclusion, the healthcare sector is on the cusp of a paradigm shift, driven by the advent of digital twins. These virtual models offer a futuristic yet tangible promise of enhanced precision, personalized care, and improved patient outcomes. As technology continues to advance, the integration of digital twins into mainstream healthcare practices will likely become not just beneficial but indispensable, reshaping the landscape of medical science and patient care for years to come.

Sustainability Efforts

As we venture into the future of digital twins and virtual assets, a significant aspect that emerges is their potential to revolutionize sustainability efforts across various industries. The concept of sustainability has long been a focal point for businesses aiming to reduce their environmental footprint, and digital twins offer innovative solutions to achieve these goals.

Digital twins enable companies to create accurate virtual replicas of physical assets, which allow for advanced monitoring, simulation, and optimization in real-time. By utilizing these digital counterparts, industries can significantly reduce waste and enhance resource efficiency. In the manufacturing sector, for instance, digital twins can simulate production processes, identifying inefficiencies and providing optimal solutions before physical implementation. This preemptive approach minimizes material waste and energy consumption, leading to a more sustainable production cycle.

In the realm of construction, digital twins offer similar benefits. Building Information Modeling (BIM) has been a breakthrough in architectural design, and the integration of digital twins takes it a step further. By creating a dynamic, data-rich model of an entire building, stakeholders can engage in more effective planning, construction, and maintenance. These models can predict potential failures, optimize energy usage, and improve lifecycle management. As a result, buildings can operate more efficiently, reducing their carbon footprint and contributing to overall environmental sustainability.

Supply chain management also stands to gain immensely from the deployment of digital twins. By mapping out the entire supply chain in a virtual environment, companies can gain deep insights into every aspect of their logistics network. This level of visibility allows managers to identify bottlenecks, predict disruptions, and optimize routes for transportation. Consequently, this reduces fuel consumption and lowers emissions, making supply chains not just more efficient, but also more eco-friendly. In addition, digital twins can facilitate the transition to a circular economy by tracking product life cycles, enabling more effective recycling and reuse strategies.

The future potential of digital twins is not limited to these immediate applications. As artificial intelligence and machine learning technologies advance, digital twins may gain predictive capabilities that further enhance sustainability efforts. For instance, AI algorithms could analyze vast amounts of data from digital twins to forecast future scenarios, enabling proactive measures that conserve resources and mitigate environmental impact. This predictive insight could be invaluable in sectors like agriculture, where optimal resource usage is critical for sustainable growth.

Despite the promising advantages, ethical considerations surrounding the use of digital twins must be addressed to ensure equitable and responsible deployment. Data privacy and security are paramount, especially as these technologies often rely on vast amounts of sensitive information. There is a need for robust policies to protect data integrity and prevent misuse. Furthermore, the digital divide poses a challenge, as not all regions or industries may have equal access to the technological infrastructure required to harness the power of digital twins. Ensuring that these advancements benefit a broad spectrum of society, rather than exacerbating existing inequalities, is crucial for their ethical integration.

In summary, digital twins present a transformative opportunity for enhancing sustainability across industries. By enabling better resource management, reducing waste, and optimizing processes, these technologies can make significant strides towards a more sustainable future. However, the journey must be navigated with careful consideration of ethical implications to ensure that the benefits are widely and fairly distributed. As we continue to innovate and push the boundaries of what is possible with digital twins, their role in shaping a sustainable, efficient, and equitable world is undeniably compelling.

Chapter 9
Challenges and Limitations.

Technical Barriers

One of the primary technical barriers in the adoption and implementation of digital twin technology lies in data integration. For a digital twin to accurately replicate its physical counterpart, it must assimilate data from various sources, including sensors, IoT devices, and external systems. This data often exists in disparate formats, generated at different times, and collected at varying scales of granularity. Harmonizing this data into a cohesive, interoperable framework poses a significant challenge. The complexity of integrating diverse datasets is compounded by the need for real-time processing and analysis to ensure the digital twin remains an up-to-date mirror of the physical reality.

Another critical technical challenge is the scalability of digital twin technology. While implementing digital twins at a small scale, such as individual machines or specific processes, is relatively manageable, scaling this to encompass entire factories, cities, or supply chains introduces numerous complications. The sheer volume of data generated by thousands of interconnected devices can overwhelm existing IT infrastructures. This necessitates advanced data management solutions, robust cloud computing services, and sophisticated networking capabilities to handle the increased load while maintaining the system's performance and reliability.

The fidelity of the digital twin, which refers to how accurately the virtual model replicates the physical object, is another technological hurdle. Creating a high-fidelity digital twin requires meticulous attention to detail and the ability to capture even minor variances in the physical object's state. Achieving this high level of detail often demands sophisticated modeling technologies and simulations, which can be computationally expensive and time-consuming. Additionally, maintaining high fidelity requires continuous data updates and monitoring, which can strain resources and infrastructure.

Cybersecurity is a paramount concern in the realm of digital twins. The interconnected nature of digital twin systems exposes them to potential cyber attacks. A breach in the security of a digital twin can have significant ramifications, both for the digital representation and its physical counterpart. Effective cybersecurity measures must be implemented to safeguard the data flowing between the physical and digital worlds. This includes securing IoT devices, ensuring secure data transmission channels, and protecting the centralized data repositories and processing facilities from unauthorized access.

Another significant barrier is the standardization of digital twin technology. As this field is still in its nascent stages, there are no universally accepted standards or best practices. This lack of standardization can lead to compatibility issues, as different organizations might use various technologies, platforms, and data formats to create and manage their digital twins. The absence of standards complicates collaboration and data sharing between organizations, which can be particularly problematic in industries that rely heavily on interconnected systems and supply chains.

Real-time data processing is a cornerstone of effective digital twin technology. However, ensuring that data is processed in real-time, or near real-time, presents its own set of challenges. The latency introduced by data transmission, processing, and feedback loops can lead to delays that reduce the effectiveness of the digital twin. Advanced computing technologies, such as edge computing and 5G networks, are being explored to mitigate these latency issues, but widespread adoption is still in the developmental phase.

Finally, the integration of artificial intelligence and machine learning into digital twins accentuates the technical barriers. While AI can enhance the predictive and prescriptive capabilities of digital twins, developing and training these algorithms require vast amounts of data and significant computational power. Ensuring that the AI models remain relevant and accurate over time, especially in dynamic environments, is a continuous and resource-intensive endeavor.

In conclusion, while the potential of digital twins is vast, the technical barriers to their implementation are substantial. Overcoming these challenges will require concerted efforts from technologists, industry leaders, and policymakers to develop robust data integration methodologies, scalable infrastructures, standardized protocols, and advanced cybersecurity measures. As these obstacles are addressed, the transformative impact of digital twins on industries and society at large will become increasingly evident.

Cost Considerations

The journey towards the widespread adoption of digital twins and virtual assets is not without its challenges, and one of the most prominent hurdles is the consideration of cost. Implementing digital twins requires substantial financial investment, which encompasses a range of expenses from initial setup to ongoing maintenance and upgrades. The initial phase involves the significant cost of hardware, software, and infrastructure necessary to create and sustain the digital twin environment. High-performance computing systems, advanced sensors, and specialized software are prerequisites that can strain even well-endowed budgets. In industries such as manufacturing or construction, where margins can be notably thin, these upfront costs can be a decisive factor in the decision-making process.

The financial commitment does not end with the

deployment of hardware and software. There are ongoing operational costs to consider, such as continuous data acquisition and integration. Digital twins need real-time data to accurately reflect their physical counterparts, which necessitates a steady influx of data streams. This requirement calls for robust data management and storage solutions, each contributing additional costs. The expenses related to ensuring data accuracy, data integrity, and cybersecurity measures further amplify the investment needed. Companies must allocate funds for staff training and the development of in-house expertise to manage and utilize digital twin technology effectively. This often means hiring specialized personnel or investing in extensive training programs for existing employees, which can be a drain on both finances and time.

Moreover, the costs associated with the digital twin lifecycle are not static. They fluctuate in response to technological advancements and market changes. Upgrading systems to keep pace with innovation or to gain a competitive edge means recurring capital expenditure. For example, sensor technology and data analytics tools are continually evolving, and staying up-to-date necessitates regular outlay. The potential for high costs in the event of system failure should also be considered. If a digital twin system experiences a malfunction, the expense of repairs, potential downtime, and lost productivity can be substantial. This risk further underscores the need for a comprehensive financial strategy to manage and mitigate these costs effectively.

Despite these considerable financial requirements, it's essential to view the cost considerations not solely as burdens but as investments with the potential for significant returns. The initial and ongoing expenses can be justified by the myriad benefits that digital twins offer. Enhanced efficiency, predictive maintenance, better decision-making capabilities, and improved product lifecycle management are just a few of the ways digital twins can generate value. By preempting issues and optimizing operations, companies can achieve substantial cost savings over time, potentially offsetting the initial investments.

For smaller companies or sectors with limited funding, creative financial strategies may be essential to leverage the benefits of digital twins without prohibitive burdens. Partnerships, shared resources, and cloud-based solutions can reduce the financial strain and make these advanced technologies accessible. Governments and industry bodies may also play a role by providing subsidies or incentives to encourage the adoption of digital technologies.

Ultimately, while cost considerations in the implementation of digital twins and virtual assets are undeniably significant, they should be balanced against the long-term gains and strategic advantages they offer. Navigating these financial challenges with foresight and adaptability can enable organizations to harness the full potential of digital twins, driving innovation and competitiveness in the rapidly evolving digital landscape.

Adoption Hurdles

Successfully integrating digital twins into existing industrial frameworks presents several significant challenges and limitations that must be thoroughly addressed for these technologies to fulfill their potential. One of the primary hurdles is the substantial initial investment required. Implementing digital twins necessitates the acquisition of advanced hardware, software, and expertise, which can be prohibitively expensive for many organizations. The cost includes not only the technology itself but also the training and development needed to make effective use of it. For smaller companies or those operating with limited financial resources, this barrier can be a substantial deterrent to adoption.

Another critical challenge is the complexity involved in accurately creating and maintaining digital twins. Crafting precise virtual models of physical assets demands a deep and often intricate understanding of both the physical and virtual realms. Ensuring that these models reflect real-time changes requires continuous data collection and analysis, imposing a demand for robust data integration frameworks and real-time processing capabilities. This complexity can strain existing IT infrastructure and necessitate significant upgrades, which in turn adds to the overall cost and effort involved.

Interoperability and standardization constitute another significant issue. The lack of universally accepted standards makes it difficult for digital twins to seamlessly integrate with existing systems and across different platforms and industries. This fragmentation can lead to inefficiencies and hinder the collaborative potential, which is one of the key benefits of digital twin technology. Without a coherent set of standards, ensuring consistency, accuracy, and reliability across various digital twin implementations becomes an arduous task.

Data privacy and security emerge as crucial concerns in the adoption of digital twins. These technologies rely heavily on the collection and analysis of vast amounts of data, often in real time. This data can include sensitive and proprietary information that, if inadequately protected, could be vulnerable to breaches or misuse. Therefore, robust security measures must be in place to safeguard this information, while at the same time ensuring that privacy concerns are adequately addressed. The challenge lies in striking a balance between leveraging data for improved efficiencies and maintaining stringent security protocols to protect it.

Resistance to change within organizations can also pose a significant hurdle. Existing workflows, processes, and mindsets are often deeply ingrained, and transitioning to a new, technology-driven paradigm can encounter significant pushback from management and staff alike. Overcoming this resistance requires not just the introduction of new technologies but also thorough change management strategies, including comprehensive education and training programs. These initiatives must articulate the long-term benefits and potential of digital twins to alleviate fears and foster a culture that embraces innovation.

Furthermore, the rapid pace of technological advancement poses its own set of challenges. The field of digital twins is continuously evolving, which means that today's cutting-edge solutions can quickly become obsolete. This dynamic landscape necessitates continuous learning and adaptability from organizations, requiring ongoing investments in skills and technology to stay at the forefront of the field. For many, the uncertainty surrounding the long-term viability and stability of the technology can be a significant deterrent to adoption.

Lastly, addressing the ethical considerations related to the deployment of digital twins is paramount. Questions surrounding data ownership, the potential for surveillance, and the broader societal implications of widespread digital replication must be thoughtfully navigated. Ethical frameworks and guidelines need to be established to ensure that the deployment of digital twin technology does not exacerbate existing inequalities or result in unintended negative consequences.

In summary, while digital twins offer tremendous promise for transforming industries through enhanced efficiencies and innovative capabilities, the road to widespread adoption is fraught with challenges. Overcoming these hurdles requires a concerted effort that includes substantial financial investment, addressing technical complexities, establishing standards, ensuring data security, managing organizational change, and navigating ethical considerations. Only by addressing these multifaceted issues head-on can the full potential of digital twins be realized within various industrial domains.

Interoperability Issues

Interoperability issues represent a significant challenge in the deployment and utility of digital twins and virtual assets. These hurdles stem from the inherent diversity of systems, platforms, and technologies employed to create and manage digital twins across different industries. Each digital twin might be designed and built using a unique combination of software and hardware, often tailored to the specific needs and intricacies of the particular industry or application. This variability can lead to significant gaps in communication and data exchange between different digital twins and the systems they interact with.

One critical issue is the lack of standardized protocols and frameworks for digital twin data exchange. As digital twins replicate increasingly sophisticated and diverse physical entities, the data they generate can vary widely in structure, format, and semantics. Without a common language or standardized method for data representation, integrating data from multiple digital twins becomes a complex and error-prone task. In the context of a smart factory, for instance, digital twins of different machines or processes might produce disparate types of data that do not seamlessly align, making comprehensive analysis and optimization difficult.

Moreover, the proprietary nature of many digital twin technologies exacerbates interoperability problems. Vendors often develop their digital twin solutions with proprietary formats and interfaces, locking users into specific ecosystems and limiting their ability to integrate with other systems. This vendor lock-in not only hampers interoperability but also restricts the flexibility and scalability of digital twin implementations. When organizations attempt to integrate digital twins from different vendors, they frequently encounter significant barriers requiring extensive customization and additional middleware to bridge these gaps.

Effective interoperability also demands robust cybersecurity measures. As digital twins often involve the real-time exchange of sensitive and critical data, ensuring secure and reliable communication channels is paramount. Diverse security protocols and standards across different digital twin solutions can complicate efforts to maintain a secure interoperable environment. Compromised security measures can lead to data breaches, operational disruptions, and even physical damage, particularly in critical sectors like healthcare and infrastructure.

Furthermore, achieving interoperability requires overcoming not just technical barriers but also organizational and cultural ones. Different stakeholders, ranging from IT and operations to engineering and management, might have varying priorities and levels of understanding regarding digital twins. Bridging these gaps necessitates comprehensive collaboration and a concerted effort to standardize practices and expectations across the board. The successful implementation of interoperable digital twins often demands a clear governance framework, with well-defined roles and responsibilities for all involved parties.

The dynamic nature of technology trends poses another layer of complexity to interoperability. As digital twin technologies evolve rapidly, keeping pace with the latest developments while ensuring compatibility with existing systems can be daunting. Continuous updates and modifications to digital twin solutions necessitate ongoing efforts to maintain interoperability. Organizations must invest in regular training and infrastructure upgrades to stay current with technological advances, further complicating interoperability efforts.

Despite these challenges, strides are being made toward improving interoperability in the world of digital twins. Industry consortia and standardization bodies are working tirelessly to develop universal standards and best practices. Initiatives like the Industrial Internet Consortium (IIC) and platforms such as the Digital Twin Consortium aim to foster a collaborative environment where stakeholders can collectively address interoperability challenges. As digital twins become more integrated into various sectors, ongoing innovation and concerted efforts toward standardization will be crucial in overcoming interoperability issues and unlocking the full potential of digital twins and virtual assets.

Chapter 10
Case Studies and Real-world Implementations.

Automotive Industry

The automotive industry has been one of the most enthusiastic adopters of digital twin technology, fundamentally transforming the way vehicles are designed, produced, and maintained. Traditional automotive design and manufacturing processes, often plagued by inefficiencies and high costs, have been revolutionized by the integration of virtual replicas. These digital twins allow engineers to simulate and analyze virtually every aspect of a vehicle's lifecycle, from initial design concepts to post-production maintenance.

One of the most significant impacts of digital twins in the automotive industry is evident in the design phase. Engineers can create highly detailed virtual models of vehicles, which can then be tested and refined without the need for physical prototypes. This not only accelerates the development process but also leads to substantial cost savings. For example, simulations can predict how different materials will affect the vehicle's performance, safety, and fuel efficiency, enabling designers to make informed decisions early in the process. As a result, car manufacturers can bring innovative vehicles to market much faster and with fewer resources.

Manufacturing processes have also benefited greatly from digital twins. Factories equipped with this technology can create an exact digital replica of the entire production line. This enables real-time monitoring and predictive maintenance, drastically reducing downtime and improving overall efficiency. For instance, if a particular machine in the production line deviates from its expected performance, the digital twin can immediately flag this anomaly. Engineers can then investigate and address the issue before it leads to costly interruptions. Moreover, these virtual models can simulate various production scenarios to optimize workflows and even reconfigure the layout of the production line for maximum efficiency.

Once vehicles roll off the production line, digital twins continue to play an essential role. Each car produced can have its own digital twin, which keeps track of the vehicle's condition and performance over time. This is particularly valuable for predictive maintenance. Instead of relying on scheduled maintenance checks, which can be inefficient and overlook potential problems, car owners and manufacturers can use data from the digital twin to predict when and what kind of maintenance will be necessary. This shift from reactive to proactive maintenance extends the lifespan of vehicles and ensures they operate at peak performance, thereby boosting customer satisfaction and loyalty.

The integration of digital twins in the automotive industry also opens up new avenues for innovation. Connected vehicles, which communicate with each other and with infrastructure, can leverage digital twin technology to enhance safety and efficiency. For example, in the case of autonomous vehicles, digital twins can simulate countless driving scenarios, helping refine the car's decision-making algorithms and improving safety measures before the vehicles even hit the road. This level of detailed simulation and analysis is crucial for the development of reliable and safe autonomous vehicles.

As digital twin technology continues to evolve, ethical considerations become increasingly important. The vast amount of data generated by these virtual models raises concerns about data security and privacy. Manufacturers must ensure that the data collected is protected and used responsibly. Additionally, there is the issue of job displacement as automation and predictive maintenance reduce the need for human intervention. Companies must balance the benefits of these technological advancements with the potential impact on their workforce, implementing strategies to reskill employees and create new job opportunities within the digital framework.

In conclusion, the automotive industry's adoption of digital twin technology represents a significant leap forward in efficiency, innovation, and customer satisfaction. By enabling detailed virtual modeling and real-time analysis, digital twins not only streamline the design and manufacturing processes but also enhance vehicle performance and longevity. As the technology continues to advance, it will be crucial to address the ethical implications to ensure a balanced and sustainable integration into the industry's future.

Aerospace Applications

In recent years, the aerospace industry has embraced digital twins to enhance various aspects of design, manufacturing, and maintenance processes. This advanced technology, which creates virtual replicas of physical systems, is revolutionizing how aerospace companies approach innovation and operational efficiency. One of the most compelling applications of digital twins in aerospace is their role in the development and testing of new aircraft models. Traditionally, designing a new aircraft involved extensive physical prototyping and testing, which was both time-consuming and costly. With digital twins, aerospace engineers can create accurate virtual replicas of proposed designs and simulate their performance under a wide range of conditions. This allows for rapid iteration, enabling engineers to identify and address potential issues long before any physical prototype is constructed. As a result, the development cycle is significantly shortened, and costs are drastically reduced.

Additionally, digital twins play a crucial role in manufacturing processes within the aerospace sector. The production of aircraft components is a highly complex task that requires extreme precision. By employing digital twins, manufacturers can monitor and optimize each step of the production process in real-time. These virtual replicas provide continuous feedback on the performance of machinery and tools, ensuring that any deviations from desired specifications are immediately detected and corrected. This leads to higher quality products, fewer defects, and reduced waste. Moreover, the ability to simulate manufacturing processes before actual production starts allows companies to identify potential bottlenecks and inefficiencies, ensuring a smoother and more efficient production line.

The maintenance and operation of aircraft also benefit greatly from the use of digital twins. By creating virtual models of individual aircraft and their components, airlines and maintenance teams can monitor the real-time health and performance of their fleets. These digital twins are continuously updated with data from sensors embedded in the aircraft, providing a comprehensive and up-to-date picture of each component's condition. Predictive maintenance, driven by digital twins, enables early detection of potential issues before they lead to costly failures or unplanned downtime. This approach not only enhances safety but also extends the lifespan of aircraft, resulting in significant cost savings for airlines.

Furthermore, digital twins offer valuable insights for optimizing flight operations. By simulating different flight scenarios, including varying weather conditions and air traffic configurations, airlines can identify the most efficient routes and altitudes, reducing fuel consumption and emissions. These simulations also help in devising strategies for emergency situations, improving overall flight safety. The ability to anticipate and mitigate potential risks before they occur adds a layer of robustness to the operational strategies employed by airlines.

The integration of digital twins in the aerospace industry raises important ethical considerations. The reliance on continuous data streams and real-time monitoring poses potential privacy and security concerns. Ensuring that data is handled responsibly and securely is paramount to maintaining trust and compliance with regulatory standards. Additionally, the shift towards automation and predictive maintenance driven by digital twins might impact the workforce, necessitating retraining programs and supportive measures for affected employees to adapt to new roles.

In conclusion, digital twins are transforming the aerospace industry by enhancing design, manufacturing, maintenance, and operational processes. The ability to create and utilize precise virtual replicas of physical systems introduces a level of efficiency and accuracy previously unattainable. As this technology continues to evolve, its applications will undoubtedly expand, driving further innovation and improvements across the aerospace sector.

Energy Sector

In the energy sector, digital twins are revolutionizing the way industries manage, monitor, and optimize their operations. As the demand for energy continues to grow, coupled with the urgent need to transition towards more sustainable practices, the implementation of digital twins presents a noteworthy paradigm shift. These virtual replicas of physical assets facilitate an unprecedented level of insight, operational efficiency, and predictive capability that was previously unimaginable.

One of the foremost applications of digital twins in

the energy sector is in the realm of power generation, particularly in the management of wind farms. Wind turbine manufacturers and operators are utilizing digital twins to mirror the physical and operational characteristics of each turbine. By collecting real-time data from sensors embedded in the turbines, digital twins can simulate the operational conditions, predict failures, and optimize maintenance schedules. This predictive maintenance approach minimizes downtime and extends the lifecycle of the turbines, significantly reducing costs and enhancing energy output. Additionally, the ability to model different operational scenarios allows operators to optimize the placement and performance of wind turbines, ultimately leading to more efficient energy production.

In the oil and gas industry, digital twins are making a substantial impact on exploration and production processes. These virtual models offer a comprehensive view of the complex infrastructure involved in drilling, extraction, and transportation. By simulating various geological conditions and operational parameters, companies can make more informed decisions, mitigate risks, and improve safety. For instance, digital twins enable the visualization of subsurface environments, allowing engineers to predict the behavior of reservoirs and optimize drilling strategies. This leads to more efficient resource extraction and reduces environmental impact. Moreover, digital twins help in planning, monitoring, and managing offshore platforms, ensuring that maintenance activities are performed only when necessary, thereby decreasing costs and minimizing disruptions.

The utilities sector, especially in power distribution and grid management, is another area where digital twins have found transformative applications. Smart grid technology, integrated with digital twins, facilitates real-time monitoring and management of electricity flow. This integration enhances the reliability and efficiency of power distribution networks. Utility companies use digital twins to simulate grid operations, predict potential faults, and develop strategies to mitigate them before they occur. For example, in the case of adverse weather conditions, digital twins can simulate the impact on power lines and infrastructure, allowing proactive measures to be taken to prevent outages. Furthermore, through the detailed analysis of performance data, digital twins help in optimizing energy consumption patterns, integrating renewable energy sources, and advancing demand response strategies.

In the transition to renewable energy, digital twins also play a vital role in the planning and execution of large-scale solar power projects. By creating a digital model of the solar farm, stakeholders can optimize the layout and orientation of solar panels to maximize energy harvest. Real-time monitoring enables the detection of performance issues, ensuring that the solar plant operates at peak efficiency. Moreover, digital twins can simulate the impact of shading, weather changes, and other environmental factors on energy production, allowing for dynamic adjustments and better energy management.

Ethical considerations in the deployment of digital twins in the energy sector revolve around data security and privacy. Given the sensitive nature of the data collected from critical infrastructure, robust cybersecurity measures are imperative to guard against potential threats. Additionally, the equitable access to these advanced technologies remains a concern, as the benefits of digital twins should ideally be accessible to a wide range of stakeholders, including smaller enterprises and developing regions.

In conclusion, the energy sector's adoption of digital twins is fostering a wave of innovation and efficiency that promises significant economic and environmental benefits. From optimizing renewable energy installations to enhancing the safety and productivity of traditional power generation and distribution, digital twins are not just a tool for improvement but a cornerstone of the energy industry's future.

Public Infrastructure

In the realm of public infrastructure, digital twins are revolutionizing how cities and governments conceive, design, and maintain critical assets. The adoption of these virtual replicas is streamlining processes, enhancing efficiency, and fundamentally transforming urban management. One of the most compelling examples of this paradigm shift is in city planning and infrastructure maintenance.

Take, for instance, the pioneering efforts of

Singapore, frequently referred to as a "Smart Nation." The city-state has developed a comprehensive digital twin of its entire urban environment. This virtual model integrates data from various sources, including satellites, drones, and ground sensors, enabling city planners and engineers to simulate and analyze multiple scenarios virtually before implementing them in the physical world. For instance, by modeling traffic flow within the digital twin, planners can identify congestion hotspots and test the impact of new road designs or traffic light configurations, all without causing real-world disruptions.

Digital twins also play a significant role in managing public utilities. Water distribution networks, for example, are notoriously complex and prone to inefficiencies and leakages. In the Netherlands, the national water authority has adopted digital twin technology to create a highly detailed model of its water system. By continuously integrating data on water usage, weather conditions, and infrastructure performance, the digital twin enables predictive maintenance, where potential issues are identified and addressed before they escalate into significant problems. This not only ensures a more reliable supply of water but also optimizes resource allocation and reduces operational costs.

Similarly, in the energy sector, digital twins are being utilized to manage the intricate networks of electrical grids. The city of Helsinki, Finland, has developed a digital twin of its power grid, which includes real-time data from smart meters, renewable energy sources such as solar panels, and traditional power plants. This comprehensive model allows operators to balance supply and demand more efficiently, predict and mitigate power outages, and integrate renewable energy sources seamlessly into the grid. Furthermore, such technology assists in planning future infrastructure upgrades by providing data-driven insights that enhance decision-making processes.

Public transport systems are another crucial area where digital twins are making a substantial impact. The City of Los Angeles has created a digital twin of its extensive public transportation network. Through this virtual model, transit authorities can simulate and optimize routes, monitor the condition of infrastructure like bridges and tunnels, and manage the scheduling and dispatching of buses and trains. This makes the public transport system more reliable and responsive to the needs of the city's residents, encouraging greater use of public transit and reducing traffic congestion and pollution.

The benefits of digital twins extend beyond operational efficiencies. They also offer robust tools for enhancing public safety and resilience. In a city prone to natural disasters, such as San Francisco, digital twins are being used to model earthquake scenarios. These models allow city officials to predict the impact of various magnitudes of earthquakes on buildings, roads, and other critical infrastructure, enabling better preparedness and more strategic allocation of emergency response resources. Additionally, by simulating the aftermath of such events, authorities can optimize recovery efforts, potentially saving lives and reducing economic losses.

Despite these promising applications, the deployment of digital twins in public infrastructure carries ethical considerations. Privacy concerns arise from the vast amounts of data collected and processed, necessitating stringent safeguards to protect individual and community privacy.

Moreover, the reliance on advanced technology must not widen the digital divide, where only well-resourced areas benefit from these innovations, leaving underprivileged communities further behind.

In conclusion, the implementation of digital twins in public infrastructure is a transformative development with far-reaching implications. By facilitating more efficient planning, maintenance, and management of urban environments, these virtual replicas are not only enhancing the livability and sustainability of cities but also preparing them to meet future challenges. However, it is essential to navigate the accompanying ethical concerns carefully to ensure that the benefits of digital twins are equitably distributed and that public trust in these technologies is maintained.

www.ingramcontent.com/pod-product-compliance
Lightning Source LLC
Chambersburg PA
CBHW052316220526
45472CB00001B/142